Wakefield Trinity RLFC

FIFTY GREAT GAMES

Wakefield Trinity RLFC

FIFTY GREAT GAMES

BY LES HOOLE

First published in Great Britain in 2004 by The Breedon Books Publishing Company Limited
Breedon House, 3 The Parker Centre, Derby, DE21 4SZ.

This paperback edition published in Great Britain in 2015 by DB Publishing,
an imprint of JMD Media Ltd

Acknowledgements

I would like to thank the following for helping with photographs and rare images from their
private collections:

Terry Kelly and Martin Grady of the Redoubt, Wakefield; Dave Makin, Raymond Fletcher
and David Hobson of the Graziers, Market Street, Wakefield; Richard Shaw Wright of Wakefield
Trinity Wildcats Rugby League Club; Harry Edgar of the *Rugby League Journal*.

Thanks also to John Clifford of JAC images and Sig Kasatkin of RL Photos for their help at
such short notice and Kay at Viz Biz Design for copying the older images.

Dianne, Verity and Ben Hoole and Cliff Pearson for their help and encouragement.

David Hinchliffe MP for his help and for writing the foreword.

I am also indebted to the countless journalists from a variety of newspapers who have written
about Wakefield Trinity over the years. Their detailed match reports and insights into the club,
its players and the games have been invaluable.

ISBN 978-1-78091-461-9

Contents

Foreword

by David Hinchliffe, Member of Parliament for Wakefield

I have a mate called George Denton, a Wakefield lad within a few months of the same age as me. He started watching Wakefield Trinity as a boy at almost exactly the same time as I did. Like me, he witnessed the great team of the 1960s and experienced the immense pride of our city in their great sporting achievements.

But, unlike me, he remembers every last detail of the numerous great matches we saw – the players, the tries and goals, the controversial refereeing decisions and even the weather. He waxes lyrical about travelling on pre-M62 winter journeys to Trinity matches on the wrong side of the Pennines as a boy in short trousers on the back of his dad's motorbike. With added lubrication, he will probably even tell you about the quality of the half-time pie.

Sadly, I have no such detailed recollection of many of the matches I have been at. Although there are some exceptions, much of my memory of past Trinity games is something of a blur, where events and incidents from different contests or even eras get mingled together. So for people like me, this book is a godsend.

I first met Les Hoole in the same Wakefield hostelry frequented by George Denton. At the time, I had read some of his previous books on rugby league and had enormous respect for his detailed knowledge of our sport. I was delighted to learn of his plans to produce this book on 50 of Trinity's greatest matches.

His unique insights into the history of the club and thorough research have enabled him to single out for discussion some of the most noteworthy games in Trinity's 131-year existence. The end result is a fascinating read and his choice of matches will no doubt provoke considerable debate among rugby league fans from several different generations.

Introduction

Wakefield Trinity Rugby League Football Club was formed in 1873 as part of the Holy Trinity Church Young Men's Society in George Street. They adopted black and blue horizontal striped shirts as their club colours and played their first games on land at Heath Common.

The club moved to Manor Field Ground near the Cathedral and then to a pitch at Elm Tree Street near the Alexandra Hotel at Belle Vue. On Easter Monday, 14 April 1879, Trinity opened their new ground and present home, Belle Vue.

Trinity were a powerful force in Rugby Union, winning the Yorkshire Cup on four occasions. At the great split in 1895, they were founder members of the Northern Union, and in 1909 won the Challenge Cup for the first time. They collected the Yorkshire Cup for the first time in 1910 and then had intermittent success which included winning the Yorkshire Cup for the second time in 1924.

A great revival took place immediately after World War Two and Trinity appeared at Wembley for the first time, defeating Wigan at Wembley in 1946 and collecting the Yorkshire Cup in 1946 and 1947.

During the late 1950s Wakefield began to nurture some of the local talent and many of the club's finest players were gradually brought into first-team football. Alongside this strategy, the club also entered the transfer market and some shrewd deals brought many great players to Belle Vue.

In the early 1960s the bold plans of the club began to come to a glorious climax and Wakefield Trinity were one of the most successful clubs in the game. Trinity won the Challenge Cup three times in four appearances and also collected the Yorkshire Cup and League trophies. In 1967 they were crowned Champions for the first time and repeated the feat the following season.

A period of rapid decline followed, with the club plagued by poor playing standards and financial problems, until in 1999 a revival saw Wakefield promoted to Super League. They have since narrowly avoided relegation several times.

Throughout their history Trinity have been involved in innumerable famous games. These 50 games selected cover all eras of Wakefield's proud past and feature famous victories against touring sides, Cup Final wins and League games. The matches feature brilliant individual performances from some of the club's finest players, as well as victories where it was the tremendous team spirit that took the club to glory.

All Blacks receive their first check

Tour match at Belle Vue, Wakefield, 23 October 1907
Wakefield Trinity 5, New Zealand 5

The first tour of England and Wales by a professional rugby team had been the idea of Albert Henry Baskerville, a rugby union forward with the Oriental club in Wellington, New Zealand. Baskerville had read avidly about the Northern Union's breakaway from the English Rugby Union and was determined to organise a tour to play the new 13-a-side code of football.

Scornfully dubbed 'The All Golds' by the New Zealand press, the tourists sailed to Australia where they defeated the New South Wales Rugby Union in three games and then set sail for their great adventure in Britain.

The Northern Union supporters in England took the party to heart the minute they arrived and the newly christened 'All Blacks' were given an inspiring reception in Leeds.

Although hardly masters of the new code the New Zealanders were experienced footballers and by the time they arrived in Wakefield for their fifth game of the gruelling 35-match schedule they were unbeaten. Their visit to Wakefield stirred the sporting public's imagination and despite heavy rain falling in the morning, a crowd of 5,800 assembled at Belle Vue for the first in what would be a long tradition of encounters against touring sides.

The Belle Vue pitch was heavy following the morning's rain, and it was Trinity who adapted quickly and smoothly to the conditions. The ample possession the forwards gained in the early scrums gave Trinity plenty of opportunities to attack but Riley and Auton both nervously knocked on in front of the line.

The All Black forwards seemed cumbersome compared to Wakefield's pack. The *Yorkshire Post* commented:

The New Zealanders pose for the press at Headingley. The All Blacks played 35 games and defeated the Northern Union 2–1 in the Test series.

> *Their forwards were slow, heavy and clumsy and once more failed to secure an equal share of the ball in the scrummages. In physique and weight the colonial forwards were obviously superior. The Wakefield men's deficiencies were, however, made good by the remarkable tenacity with which they played on the ball. They were clever in gaining possession, and in the loose they simply gave the heavy New Zealand forwards no rest.*

Wakefield took the lead when full-back Metcalfe kicked a penalty following an incident of obstruction. Just before half-time clever passing from Slater and McPhail prised open a gap for Lynch to score a try which Metcalfe failed to convert.

The mauling they had suffered in the first half prompted the tourists to rearrange their line-up in the second, but the movements did little to help get their renowned back division into the play. The All Blacks adopted a kick and rush policy which, with Wakefield playing one of their finest games of the season, was doomed from the outset.

The game was hard fought in the second half, as one newspaper report noted:

> *The match may best be likened unto a keen Yorkshire Cup tie. Not that it was roughly fought, though towards the close little was asked or given and boot toes were flourished with little discrimination.*

Penalties were awarded with alarming frequency by the referee and it was from one awarded for obstruction that Dally Messenger kicked a goal for the All Blacks' first score.

Shortly after, a powerful forward rush by the tourists brought play near to the Wakefield line where Byrne picked up and passed to Smith, who swerved round several defenders before passing to Rowe, who scored in the corner. Messenger failed with the conversion attempt.

With the contest locked at five points each, both sides attacked frantically and play constantly swept the length of the field. Defences held firm, however, and neither side made the breakthrough: the game ended all square with Wakefield becoming the first side to halt the tourists' run of victories.

Wakefield's play had been exceptional. To draw against a touring side was a great feat, as the *Yorkshire Post* commented:

> *The Trinitarians probably played their best game of the season. They had a big task to essay and right gallantly did they attempt it. The best passing of the game was provided by the Wakefield backs and the manner in which Slater, Newbould, McPhail, Ward, Lynch and Booth combined was almost a revelation even to the regular supporters of the Trinity club.*

Wakefield Trinity

Metcalfe, Booth, Lynch, Ward, McPhail, Slater, Newbould, J. Taylor, G. Taylor, Auton, Riley, Beaumont, Parkes

Try: Lynch

Goal: Metcalfe

New Zealand

Turtill, Lavery, Smith, Rowe, Wynyard, Messenger, Gleeson, Mackrell, Dunning, Tyler, Pearce, Byrne, Tyne

Try: Rowe

Goal: Messenger

Attendance: 5,800

Hunslet's fourth defeat

League match at Parkside, Hunslet, 1 February 1908
Hunslet 5, Wakefield Trinity 9

In 1906 the Northern Union made the innovative decision to discard two forwards and reduce teams to 13 players. The radical move that was to change the shape and tactics of the game was brilliantly embraced by Hunslet and, a season after the new rules were introduced, the south Leeds club astounded the Northern Union world by sweeping all before them to win each of the four trophies available. It was an astounding feat, utilising tactics that were based around the kicking abilities of their veteran captain, Albert Goldthorpe, and a fearsome set of forwards who became known as the 'Terrible Six'.

Hunslet began their season in style by winning their first 23 games, which included the very first Yorkshire Cup Final, before a surprise defeat away to Hull Kingston Rovers stunned the Parksiders. Two defeats at Salford and lowly placed newcomers Merthyr Tydfil followed, then it was back to south Leeds to face Wakefield Trinity in a match that all the pundits believed would steady the team and see a return to the victories of the first part of the season.

Trinity, who were 10 points behind Hunslet having lost eight games, had other thoughts about the game and from the kick-off the Wakefield forwards played a powerful and lively game that beat the famous 'Terrible Six' at their own strategy.

Major of the *Leeds Mercury*, writing about the match, reported:

> *The Trinitarian scrummages had the best of matters, and their bustling tactics quite disconcerted the home pack. They got possession frequently and instantly the ball came out, while on the other side its progress was very slow and Albert Goldthorpe at the base of the pack had many a dreary wait.*

Hunslet used the strong wind that gusted across Parkside well in the first half and within

Tommy Newbould and Fred Smith, the opposing half-backs, sit together on the far right of the front row in this tour trial line up.

20 minutes C. Ward had crossed Wakefield's line for a try following a clever bout of passing between Goldthorpe and Eagers. The usually reliable Goldthorpe failed with the conversion attempt but soon after dropped a goal to increase the Parksiders' lead to five points.

Wakefield responded well and a smart passing movement by Slater and Bennett prised open the Hunslet defence to allow Sidwell to romp over the line for a try in the corner. Metcalfe failed with the conversion attempt.

Wakefield's try rocked the Hunslet side and, sensing their hosts' discomfort, Trinity swept forward with a series of passing movements that began to pierce gaps galore in the Parksiders' lines of defence. The brief but unrelenting pressure gave Wakefield exactly what they needed when the ever-alert Bennett pounced on a loose ball and made good ground before transferring to Slater who swept in for an unconverted try in the corner.

The teams broke at half-time with Wakefield holding a well-deserved 6–5 lead. Shortly after the restart a passing move involving Slater and Newbould gave wing man Bennett the opening to score the third try of the afternoon which gave Trinity a 9–5 lead.

Wakefield's second-half tactics demoralised Hunslet and the home side were beaten throughout the 40 minutes, as Metcalfe, Slater and Newbould constantly used the strong wind to send the ball sailing deep into Hunslet's half of the pitch. The Parksiders struggled to recover from the punishing kicks and Trinity's domination of the scrums, and soon abandoned passing

HUNSLET FALL AT HOME.

THE REFEREE LECTURES THE CROWD.

Scorers:—Wakefield: Sidwell, Slater, and Bennett, tries.

Hunslet—Ward, try; A. E. Goldthorpe, goal.

Quite a change has come over the once all-conquering team of Hunslet, and Wakefield has added another defeat to those already sustained. Playing on their own ground, it was thought that Hunslet would find their true form again, but such was not the case, and the deterioration in their play was painfully manifest. There was a laxity and slackness which suggested staleness, and this perhaps was the cause of the weakness. They had a couple of good men away in the persons of Batten and Walter Goldthorpe, and this tended to disorganisation in the three-quarter line.

The forwards, though Jukes and Randall were absent, were practically at full strength, and yet the Trinitarian scrimmagers had the best of matters, and their bustling tactics quite disconcerted the home pack. They got possession frequently, and instantly the ball came out, while on the other side its progress was very slow, and Albert Goldthorpe at the base of the pack had many a wait. Once in the second half we ... mnie of the old-time fire and dash, ... the same

The match as reported in a newspaper of the time.

movements in favour of forward rush tactics. Their ploy looked dangerous and Wakefield floundered a little until they made the clever tactical decision to withdraw Auton from the scrums to aid the defence.

Wakefield's famous victory was marred towards the end of the game when a section of the Hunslet crowd took exception to some of referee Clegg's decisions and began jeering him. The barracking continued until the official halted the game and went over to rebuke the highly partisan crowd.

Hunslet

Place, Farrar, Haycox, Eagers, C. Ward, A. Goldthorpe, Smith, Wilson, Brookes, W. Wray, Walsh, Smales, Higson

Try: C. Ward

Goal: A. Goldthorpe

Wakefield Trinity

Metcalfe, Bennett, McPhail, Sidwell, Lynch, Slater, Newbould, Crossland, Taylor, Auton, Walton, Beaumont, McDonnell

Tries: Sidwell, Slater, Bennett

Attendance: 4,000

The Kangaroos beaten again

Tour match at Belle Vue, 19 December 1908
Wakefield Trinity 20, Australia 13

There was no mistaking the superiority of Wakefield Trinity in their match with the Kangaroos at Belle Vue. They were a fine and well-balanced team. Their forward play was much more effective than that of the Colonials. The half-backs proved smart and resourceful and the three-quarters were at the top of their form.

That was the verdict on the game from the *Yorkshire Post*.

The first Australian Kangaroos to tour Britain embarked on a punishing 45-match tour which saw them travel the length and breadth of the country. They played games as far apart as London, Glasgow and South Wales, winning 17, losing 22 and drawing six of their games, which included every Northern Union club and a variety of representative sides.

By the time they arrived at Belle Vue the tourists had lost just five of their games; they had defeated Lancashire and Yorkshire and had drawn 22–22 with the Northern Union in the first Test match at Park Royal, London.

Always anxious about the financial aspect of the tour, the Australians had insisted that the admission fee for their games be one shilling and this had a bearing on the poor gate of 3,000 at Wakefield.

Trinity were at full strength for the game, half-back Slater returning to the team having been out for seven weeks following an injury he picked up in the Yorkshire–Lancashire game at Salford in October. The tourists rested their influential three-quarters Bolewski and Devereux

15

and played the great Dally Messenger at right-centre.

Messenger had toured with the New Zealanders the previous season and had opposed Trinity at Belle Vue. His worth to the Australians was immeasurable. As the *Yorkshire Post* commented:

> *Messenger was, as usual, the Kangaroos' star and had he not been playing the Colonials would have looked a moderate lot.*

The tourists began the game with a strong attack which ended abruptly when Messenger missed a penalty attempt with a poor kick at goal. Wakefield responded well, and when Lynch made a mark Metcalfe struck the post with the goal attempt. Soon after, Slater set the Trinity backs in motion and a clever round of passing ended in a series of scrums near the tourists' try-line. The Wakefield forwards heeled cleanly from one of these scrums and Newbould scooped up the ball and dashed through some slack defence to score between the posts. Metcalfe had no difficulty in adding the two points.

The Kangaroos were undaunted by the score and mounted a series of strong attacking moves with some slick passing movements. The tourists were pressing towards the Wakefield line when Messenger threw a long pass towards Frawley, allowing Auton to nip in and intercept the ball. He pounded forward for half the length of the field and just as the chasing pair of Frawley and Deane were closing him down he fired a superbly timed pass to Bennett, who easily outstripped the Australians to score a sensational try. Metcalfe converted and Trinity were 10–0 up.

The first Kangaroos to tour Britain. On the far right of the back row is Albert Rosenfield, who signed for Huddersfield and later played for Wakefield.

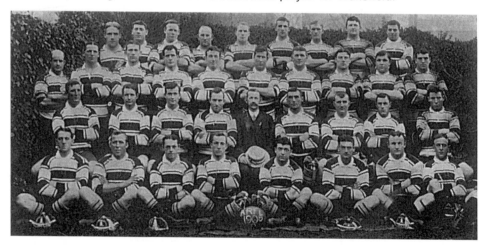

Within three minutes the tourists struck back. Anlezark, Halloway and Dean combined well to give the ball to Messenger; the centre gained ground and then transferred brilliantly to Heidke, who squeezed in at the corner for a try. Messenger's class told when he converted from a very difficult position.

Shortly before the break Sidwell completely outwitted the defence and scored near the posts. On-form full-back Metcalfe landed his third goal.

Early in the second half Messenger landed a fine penalty goal and then passed well to Frawley for the wing man to score an unconverted try. But the tourists' revival was brief. Trinity swept forward and from a scrum Newbould darted through for a try which Metcalfe converted.

Shortly before the end Walsh took advantage of Wakefield's complacency and rounded Metcalfe to score a try which Messenger failed to convert. It was the final score of a hugely entertaining game, which once again saw Wakefield hold their own against the might of a touring side.

Wakefield Trinity

Metcalfe, Bennett, Lynch, Sidwell, Simpson, Slater, Newbould, J. Taylor, Auton, G. Taylor, Crosland, Parkes, Beaumont

Tries: Newbould 2, Bennett, Sidwell

Goals: Metcalfe 4

Australia

Morton, Frawley, Messenger, Dean, Heidke, Halloway, Anlezark, Walsh, McCabe, Pearce, Courtney, Abercrombie, O'Malley

Tries: Heike, Frawley, Walsh

Goals: Messenger 2

Attendance: 3,000

The Cup comes to Wakefield

Challenge Cup Final at Headingley, 20 April 1909
Hull 0, Wakefield Trinity 17

Hull were so anxious to win the Challenge Cup in 1909 that when the team arrived in Leeds for the final they were put to bed for two to three hours in preparation for the game. Wakefield, on the other hand, made no such provisions and it was said that some of the team had been at work all week in the pit.

Trinity's good honest preparations obviously worked wonders, as they *'played well to a man and caused Hull to be a broken and dispirited team before the interval.'* From the kick-off, Trinity's forwards dominated the game and in the scrummages they excelled. Behind the scrum was Slater, the captain, whose *'boundless energy fired the whole of his team with energy.'*

Wakefield attacked from the outset, and after five minutes of play Newbould got hold of the ball in a scrummage near the Hull line and, after tricking Wallace with a dummy pass, scrabbled over to score Trinity's first points. Later Slater carved open the Hull defence with a long pass to Sidwell, who transferred quickly to Bennett, who dived over the line in the corner.

In the second half Trinity scored three further tries and Metcalfe kicked a goal. Sidwell and Bennett combined well to put Crosland over and Bennett scored his second try from a scrum.

Despite their almost total control Trinity continued to attack aggressively and at times the play became so keen that cautions were handed out on both sides. The final score came from Simpson, who notched up Wakefield's fifth try after making a great catch from a long cross-field kick.

At the final whistle the presentation was made by Mrs Nicholls, the wife of the president of the Northern Union. Slater, the Wakefield captain, took the cup:

Trinity's cup-winning team and officials pose with the tram car that toured Wakefield to celebrate the 'Dreadnowts' famous victory.

> *... and quaffed the wine it contained amid great cheering. Slater, covered in mud, said it was a great honour to win the cup and he was very sorry for Hull in their defeat. If there is one team we like to meet it is Hull because they play the passing game, the game that should be played.*

On returning home the Wakefield team had a great reception. The *Yorkshire Post* covered the journey of Trinity and the cup:

> *They left Headingley shortly after six o'clock in an illuminated car which bore several mottoes such as 'Dreadnowts is coming' and 'its 22 years sin'.*
>
> *All the way through Leeds and Hunslet crowds lined the streets and, at Lofthouse Park, the car was met by the Rutland Mills Brass Band and a triumphant procession to Wakefield was formed. A tremendous crowd greeted the victors at Newton bar, and amid terrific cheering the car made its way slowly through the town to the Bull Ring and then down Kirkgate to the Alexandra Hotel at Belle Vue.*

Dinner was served, speeches were made and then, with the band still in attendance, the team made its way through the streets of Wakefield in a charabanc to accept the adulation of their fans.

Wakefield Trinity

Metcalfe, Bennett, Lynch, Sidwell, Simpson, Slater, Newbould, Crosland, Auton, Taylor, Walton, Kershaw, Beaumont

Tries: Simpson, Newbould, Bennett 2, Crosland

Goal: Metcalfe.

Hull

Taylor, Dechan, Connell, Cotterall, E. Rogers, Anderson, Wallace, Boylen, Herridge, Britton, Carroll, Holder, Havelock

Attendance: 23,587

A contemporary sketch of the game's action.

A triumph for the Wakefield forwards

Yorkshire Challenge Cup Final at Headingley, 3 December 1910
Huddersfield 2, Wakefield Trinity 8

Wakefield won the Yorkshire Challenge Cup for the first time with a superb display of teamwork that prompted the *Yorkshire Post* to comment that they were:

> *... a team remarkable not for any outstanding brilliance of one particular player, but for the inclusion of men who play wholeheartedly, and with a tenacity of purpose, which in the end is bound to reap its reward.*

Trinity had received a bye in the first round and began the campaign with a 42–16 demolition of Northern Union newcomers Coventry at Belle Vue. In the semi-final they defeated Hull 11–0, again at Belle Vue.

Huddersfield were the Cup-holders, having beaten Batley 21–0 in the final at Headingley, and Bramley, Dewsbury and Hull Kingston Rovers on their way there. Wakefield were at the top of the Northern Union League table with just one defeat in the 11 games they had played. It was Huddersfield who were the favourites, however, despite having lost eight matches.

It was apparent from the outset that Wakefield's forwards were far superior to Huddersfield's lumbering front rank and, taking full advantage of a strong east wind, the Trinitarians embarked upon a series of loose rushes. The *Leeds Mercury* had this to say about their play:

> *The Wakefield forwards were far too good in scrummaging play and they showed even greater superiority in the loose. They were always on the ball, and their fast*

following up and sure tackling was the main factor in bringing about the victory of their side.

Newbould, Trinity's international half-back, realised his forwards' strength over Huddersfield and this dictated his tactics behind the scrum. He decided against opening the game out to his capable backs and relied on a succession of short kicks for his forwards to chase.

When Huddersfield's New Zealand centre Wrigley was penalised for obstruction, Metcalfe carefully lined up his shot from 40 yards out to send the ball clean over the bar. Then, from a scrum almost on the Huddersfield line, George Taylor picked up the ball and dashed over for a try.

Shortly before the interval Huddersfield began to string a series of movements together and Kitchen and Wagstaff had some fine runs. Huddersfield's clever three-quarters looked dangerous whenever they had the ball in their hands but Wakefield's robust tackling stopped their progress before they became dangerous.

The pace of the game increased considerably in the second half and the Wakefield forwards made their presence felt, their repeated rushes to the Huddersfield line causing havoc in the Fartowners' defence. Kitchen and Wagstaff, though, played a fine game against the might of the Trinity pack, their heroic and daring saves at the feet of the forwards stopping many certain tries.

With 15 minutes to play, Bartholomew, the Huddersfield full-back, blundered badly when attempting to field a high punt. The ball was picked up by Lynch, whose wide pass to Simpson released him for a sprint over the Huddersfield line, easily outstripping their defending players. Metcalfe failed with the conversion attempt.

Huddersfield rallied in the last few minutes of the game and their backs began to make several advances into the Wakefield half. From one of these attacks Wakefield were caught offside and Wrigley kicked a fine penalty.

It was the final score of the game; Wakefield won a hard fought contest and were awarded the Yorkshire Challenge Cup for the first time.

Although the foundations of the victory were laid by the magnificent work of the forwards, Wakefield's backs played their part too and The *Leeds Mercury* commented:

> *The Wakefield backs tackled and fielded magnificently and Simpson, at left-wing three-quarter, was very clever in snapping up chances. The Wakefield men would have won by a bigger margin had their backs emulated the Huddersfield style, for they had a least four chances to one of opening out passing movements.*

Huddersfield

Bartholomew, Rosenfeld, Wrigley, Wagstaff, Kitchen, Grey, Davies, Ainley, Byrne, Clarke, Gronow, Mellor, Sherwood

Goal: Wrigley

Wakefield Trinity

Metcalfe, Bennett, Poynton, Lynch, Simpson, Newbould, Sidwell, Auton, G. Taylor, J. Taylor, Walton, Crossland, Kershaw

Tries: Taylor, Simpson

Goals: Metcalfe

Attendance: 19,000

The programme cover and teams for the Yorkshire Cup Final at Headingley.

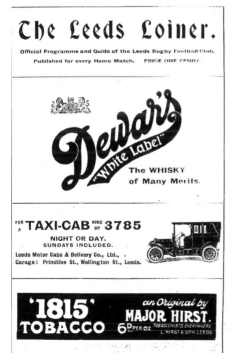

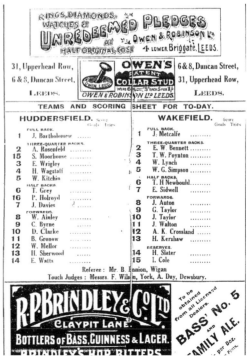

Warrington's Waterloo at Wakefield

Challenge Cup third round at Belle Vue, 28 March 1912
Wakefield Trinity 10, Warrington 5

Trinity's 1912 Challenge Cup campaign began with a 10–2 victory over Leeds at Belle Vue, and a 13–2 win at Keighley's Lawkholme Lane. The third round draw gave Wakefield a trip to Wilderspool to face Warrington.

Wakefield had won 17 of their 27 league games and were firm favourites to beat the 'Wire-pullers', who were 11 points behind Trinity in the League table.

Trinity took control of the game from the kick-off and did everything but cross the Warrington line, their finishing being far from effective. This was in part due to their own play, but also showed the strength of the Warrington defence. As the *Yorkshire Post* commented:

> *Whilst Poynton played a great game for Wakefield, Renwick and Dickenson were always prominent in upsetting many a pre-arranged scheme between Newbould, Slater and the Wakefield back line.*

Slater, Newbould and Auton, the prime architects of Warrington's defeat.

In the second half Warrington's persistence finally gave them the lead when wing man Renwick charged down a clearance kick and easily beat Smith, the Wakefield full-back, in the chase to touch down. The score against them shocked Trinity into action and with just five minutes to play, a solid passing movement gave Poynton an unconverted try to force a replay at Belle Vue.

Wakefield made two changes for the replay, bringing reserve full-back Land – *'a strapping, smart and clever player'* – in for the injured Smith and Kershaw – *'a useful emergency man'* – into the three-quarter line up for Lynch.

Warrington, who had earned the unique distinction of drawing all three of their opening Challenge Cup ties, made two changes in an attempt to strength their forces. Tilley was drafted in at full-back in place of McIntyre and the stronger Creevey took the place of Jordan at half-back.

Trinity began the game at a searing pace, seemingly anxious to finish the job started at Wilderspool as quickly as possible, and were soon pressing deep into the Warrington defences. The players were over-eager, however, and many of their attacks broke down at crucial times when jittery and uneven play led to possession and ground lost. The *Leeds Mercury* reported:

> *It did not take one long to be convinced that the Trinitarians were the better team; but it was annoying to their supporters to find them literally throwing away chances owing to over-eagerness and carelessness.*

In the first five minutes two superb chances to open the scoring were lost when first Fellowes, then Newbould kept hold of the ball with total disregard for the presence of colleagues. Wakefield finally opened the scoring in the 40th minute when Newbould kicked a penalty goal.

The second half opened with another torrid onslaught from Wakefield and it was again clear that they were by far the better side. The *Leeds Mercury* again:

> *It was in the rear department that the 'wire-drawers' were out-classed, and the only two men who were really first class were Daineth and Renwick. Newbould and Slater, although they have played better games, were too much for the opposing halves, and Poynton was also much in evidence. But the best back on the field was undoubtedly Kershaw who played a fine game, both on the attack and on the defence. He was the life and soul of his side.*

The pressure exerted on Warrington brought a try early in the half. From a scrum Slater passed to Newbould, who launched a towering cross-field kick which was gathered in by Simpson. The wing man had just enough space – and pace – to win the try.

Taylor missed the difficult place kick, but minutes later Trinity were 10–0 up when Slater once again transferred to Newbould. This time Newbould held onto the ball long enough to draw in the Warrington defence before laying off to Simpson to make the last few yards. Taylor kicked the conversion.

Warrington were far from finished, however, and their forwards began to put pressure on the Wakefield line. From a forward rush Woodburn scored a try from which Renwick kicked a neatly weighted conversion.

It was the final score of the game. Trinity went on to the Challenge Cup semi-final and were defeated 17–0 by Oldham at Wheater's Field, Broughton.

TRIUMPHANT TRINITY.

WARRINGTON'S WATERLOO AT WAKEFIELD.

Scorers:—Wakefield: Simpson (2) tries; Newbould and Taylor, goals.
Warrington.—Woodburn, try; Renwick, goal.

Warrington, who have had the distinction of having played a drawn game in each of the three rounds of the Northern Union Cup Competition, visited Wakefield with the fixed determination of meeting their Oldham friends in the semi-final round of the competition, and with the object of strengthening their forces they put Tilley at full back in place of McIntyre, and Creevey at half back instead of Jordan. One cannot find much fault with Tilley's play, but the Warrington selectors must now admit that Creevey was not an improvement on Jordan, who played a good game at Warrington. Creevey, to say the least of it, was disappointing.

Wakefield were compelled to make two important alterations in their team owing to Smith (full back) and Lynch (centre three-quarter) being injured at Wilderspool; but the substitution of Land and Kershaw certainly did not weaken the team. It was a capital "gate" for mid-week, and about 10,000 people—the receipts being £234 6s.—witnessed a game which was strenuously contested, but which did not produce the best class of football. Cup-tie contests, for some reason or other, very rarely do.

CHANCES MISSED.

It did not take one long to be convinced were the better team;

Wakefield Trinity

Land, Fellowes, Kershaw, Poynton, Simpson,

Slater, Newbould, Auton, Crosland, Burton,

Beattie,

Taylor, Walton

Tries: Simpson 2

Goals: Newbould, Taylor

Warrington

Tilley, Woodburn, Renwick, Dickinson,

McIntyre, McCreevey, Dainteth, Shugars,

Thomas, Arnold, Chester, Trantor, Skelhorne

Try: Woodburn

Goal: Renwick

Attendance: 10,000

One newspaper's view of the game.

Dramatic defeat of Leeds

Challenge Cup second round at Belle Vue, 14 March 1914
Wakefield Trinity 9, Leeds 8

At the end of the first 40 minutes of stirring cup-tie football, and in view of a Leeds performance of real quality, particularly from their back line, Trinity looked doomed to defeat. They were six points adrift and a man short.

Wakefield had started the game well enough, their formidable pack of forwards gaining ample possession from the scrums and Lynch, Kershaw and Abbot playing well in defence. But although severely limited for possession, when Leeds did gain custody of the ball, their speedy backs were a constant threat to the Trinity defence.

On the half-hour the visitors took the lead when Campbell received the ball from Ganley close to the halfway line and made a superb mazy run, dodging half a dozen Wakefield defenders and outpacing Poynton and Land to touch down in the corner.

Stacey missed the conversion attempt, but a minute later was involved in an incident which led to the Loiners' second try. The Leeds wing man made a dashing run down the touch line and, when confronted by Land, he punted the ball over the head of the Wakefield full-back, only to be *'so palpably obstructed that the referee had no hesitation in giving Leeds a try, which was not improved on.'*

Tempers rose, and just before half time, following a period of loose discipline on both sides, Newbould was singled out by the touch judge and sent off by referee Jones of Widnes.

Wakefield resumed the game with five forwards, Johnson going into the three-quarter line and Howarth to half-back. To the amazement of the crowd Leeds also made a tactical change by pulling Ward from the scrum to reinforce their three-quarters.

Lynch and Crossland.

It was a strange decision; the visitors were six points in front, playing a team of 12 men, and had struggled for most of the first half to both gain possession and contain the Trinity six. With Ward absent, Wakefield's five-man pack was more than a match for the Leeds forwards and they continued to control the scrums. The *Yorkshire Post* commented:

> *Leeds only got possession of the ball half a dozen times from the scrummages in the second half, it will be seen how ill advised it was to have withdrawn any of the scrummaging power. The withdrawing of Ward simply put the reins into Wakefield's hands.*

Trinity attacked persistently and pulled a goal back when Land let fly with a left-footed drop goal attempt that, to everyone's surprise, sailed beautifully over the bar.

Stacey cancelled the points out when he landed a fine penalty and once again Trinity were six points behind. In the final 20 minutes, Wakefield's forwards took a grip on the game and attacked the Leeds line almost at will. Poynton charged an attempted clearance kick near the Leeds line and with no Leeds player near him strolled over for an easy try which was converted by Kershaw.

The visitors were demoralised, as Trinity crowded their attack and pinned Leeds to their own line for the final onslaught. Johnson missed the chance to finish things when, from a brilliant pass from Land, he knocked on going over the Leeds try line. The inevitable came a minute later when Stacey, under great pressure, carelessly kicked directly into the hands of

Crossland, who 'marked' at a spot seven or eight yards within the Leeds half.

Trinity's young forward Beattie, *'who never until a week ago had been entrusted with such kick,'* was given the ball. The Scotsman calmly placed the ball on the halfway line and with a tremendous, towering kick sent the ball sailing through the posts to give Wakefield a dramatic one-point victory.

Wakefield Trinity

Land, Abbott, Lynch, Poynton, Howarth, Newbould, Kershaw, Dixon, Crossland, Beattie, Johnson, E. Parkin, Burton

Try: Poynton

Goals: Land, Kershaw, Beattie

Leeds

Lewis, W.H. Davies, Campbell, W.A. Davies, Stacey, Sanders, Ganley, Webster, Harrison, Sutton, Mirfield, Godward, Ward

Tries: Campbell, Stacey

Goal: Stacey

Attendance: 12,000

NORTHERN UNION CUP-TIES.

SECOND ROUND.

WAKEFIELD TRINITY v. LEEDS: HOME TEAM'S DRAMATIC VICTORY.

With all the odds against them, Wakefield Trinity succeeded in turning the tables upon Leeds in a most exciting Cup-tie on the Belle Vue ground. A crowd of 12,000 spectators witnessed the match—the gate receipts amounted to £309—and when Wakefield at half-time were six points down and were a man short, owing to the sending off of Newbould, it seemed almost certain that Leeds would on this occasion prove successful. It was the home forwards who turned the tables in the second half by their strong scrummaging and robust rushing tactics; and Leeds contributed to their own downfall by withdrawing Ward from the forwards to assist in the defence.

The run of the play was strangely uneven, for whilst Leeds had much the best of it during the first half when both teams were at full strength, it was Wakefield, with a numerical disadvantage, who made the running afterwards. Leeds was never so successful in getting possession of the ball as their opponents, but whenever the visiting backs were set going they showed a much superior smartness and finish to the home lot. In spite of the sound tackling of Lynch, Kershaw, and Abbott, the Leeds backs were often dangerous, and Stacey on one occasion had "hard lines" in not scoring at the corner. Finally after half-an-hour's play, Leeds took the lead through the brilliant individualism of Campbell, who after receiving the ball from Ganley at half-way, dodged past half-a-dozen of his opponents, and beating Poynton and Land by his superior pace, scored a magnificent try. Stacey failed to add the goal points, but the latter player was himself the means of a second try being allowed to Leeds. He had made a dashing run down the touch

A contemporary report of Wakefield's triumph over Leeds.

Trinitarians again beat Lancashire cracks

Challenge Cup third round at Belle Vue, 21 March 1914
Wakefield Trinity 9, Wigan 6

The last-minute defeat of Leeds in the second round of the Challenge Cup had given Wakefield great hope and confidence for the difficult game with Wigan.

The cherry-and-whites were second in the league table and had won 22 of their 28 games. They had defeated Bramley and Runcorn in the previous rounds and were favourites to beat Wakefield with ease. The *Leeds Mercury* reported:

> *There was no comparison between the respective backs. On the Wakefield side there were two young half-backs – J. Parkin and Howarth – who only a short time ago were playing intermediate football, and they were opposed to two men of experience and ability in the persons of Welshmen Johnny Thomas and Owens. In addition to this in Wakefield's three-quarter line were Johnson, a forward, and Abbott, who has a great deal to learn before he can be regarded as a wing three-quarter for a first class team.*

Trinity started in sensational fashion and were five points in the lead after just four minutes of play. Lynch had made a dramatic burst down the field before conceding a forward pass. Wigan's Johnny Thomas then attempted to mark on his own line and, failing this, threw a casual pass to Jenkins. Crossland needed no invitation to pounce on the loose ball over the line, and Kershaw converted with ease.

It was the confidence-boosting start Wakefield needed and their forwards soon began to monopolise the scrums and loose play. Midway through the half, Jonty Parkin broke clear and

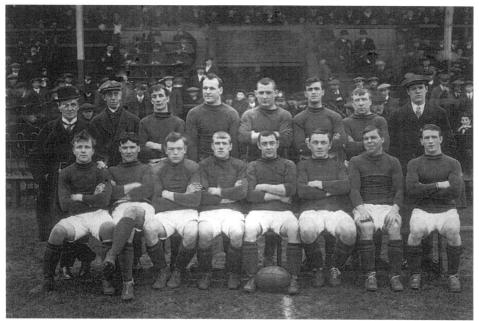

A Trinity team group from the 1913-14 season. On the far left of the front row is a young Jonty Parkin in his first season of first-team football. On the back row, second from the right, is Tommy 'Trapper' Newbould and in the centre, with the ball at his feet, is the captain, Herbert Kershaw.

Johnny Thomas had to race across the field to knock the ball into touch near the corner. From the scrum the ball was whipped across to Land who, from a position on the '25' line, dropped a brilliant goal. Ten minutes later Beattie extended the lead to nine points with a goal from a mark just inside his own half.

The power of Trinity's play and the points they scored confused Wigan and, although they made every effort to move the ball out wide, their efforts were constantly thwarted by the Wakefield defence.

Shortly before half-time a rare Wigan attack beat the Wakefield defence:

> *Jenkins scooped up the ball and after Johnny Thomas and Francis had handled,*
> *Miller passed inside to Walford who completed a pleasing effort.*

Ten minutes into the second half Wigan crossed the Trinity line again, when Seeling charged down a clearance kick from Jonty Parkin to score a rather fortunate try.

Wigan now began to launch a series of onslaughts on the Wakefield line and only some desperate defending kept them out. The *Leeds Mercury* commented:

> *Wakefield played their usual plucky, determined, and robust game. The success of*
> *the Belle Vue men must be attributed in a great measure to the splendid play of*
> *their forwards. Not content with working hard in the packs, they did their share in*
> *open play, and their activity helped in breaking-up the combination of the Wigan*
> *backs.*

Wakefield held firm and their *'local talent and true Yorkshire grit'* kept Wigan from scoring.

In the semi-final at Rochdale, Wakefield and Broughton Rangers drew 3–3. Trinity won the replay at Huddersfield 5–0 to set up an encounter with Hull and a repeat of the 1909 Challenge Cup Final.

In a major rebuilding exercise, Hull had scoured the Northern Union world for players and had assembled a powerful team littered with English and Australian internationals. Trinity played well in the final at Halifax but the might and class of Hull told and the 'Third Porters' defeated Wakefield 6–0.

———

Wakefield Trinity

Land, Abbott, Lynch, Poynton, Johnson, Howarth, J. Parkin, Dixon, Crossland, Beattie, Kershaw, E. Parkin, Burton

Try: Crossland

Goals: Kershaw, Land, Beattie.

Wigan

G. Thomas, Curwen, Jenkins, Walford, Miller, Owens, J. Thomas, Seeling, Ramsdale, Francis, Coldrich, Silcock, Richards

Tries: Walford, Seeling

Attendance: 12,000

Kingston Rovers' new ground

League match at Craven Park, Hull, 2 September 1922
Hull Kingston Rovers 0, Wakefield Trinity 3

The 1922–23 season was the first played under the new title of the Rugby Football League, the Northern Union title with its Victorian roots discarded.

Wakefield had the honour of playing in the very first game at Craven Park, Hull Kingston Rovers' new ground. Both sides were part of a procession from Paragon Station in the centre of Hull to the new ground at Holderness, and the Lord Mayor of Hull kicked off.

Kingston Rovers played their giant South African forward George Van Rooyen, *'who without distinguishing himself, played a strong game. At least one Wakefield forward will remember his first meeting with the colonial.'*

The match started slowly and for most of the first half both sides were subdued. Wakefield had the better of the first 40 minutes, with the *Wakefield Express* commenting:

> *Clever open forward play was interspersed with capital combination on the part of the backs, and Parkin getting possession of the ball exhibited rare judgement.*

Osborne and Pollard both failed with penalty kicks and the teams turned round at half-time scoreless. Fifteen minutes into the second half and, following a period of pressure from Kingston Rovers, Trinity struck:

> *Parkin got possession from a scrummage in midfield, and at once darted away. He cut cleverly through with Siswick in attendance, the transfer was made, and Siswick finished his run with a judicious punt, the ball going in the direction of*

A caricature of Albert Rosenfield, the Australian wing man who scored the first try at Hull Kingston Rovers' new ground. Rosenfield began his career with Huddersfield and moved to Wakefield in 1921. His amazing record of 80 tries during the 1913–14 season seems unlikely to be ever beaten.

the line. Rosenfield followed up, and diving for the ball, beat Harris and Osborne, and scored a splendid try.

It was a superb sprint from the veteran Australian and his fitness prompted the *Wakefield Express* to say:

The colonial reproduced his best form, which shows what can be achieved by proper training. Rosenfield's example might well be copied by younger members.

Pollard made a good attempt to convert from a difficult angle.

The Robins rallied well and the final 10 minutes of the game were played in the Trinity half, with Wakefield holding on for a famous victory.

Wakefield had struggled throughout the game to gain possession from the scrums and had tried three hookers during the match. In the loose the forwards excelled and their tackling was far more effective than the Kingston Rovers' pack. Yet it was in the half-back position that Trinity really looked supreme:

... Rogers and Parkin outgeneraling McGlone and McGiever. Rogers made the most of the opportunities which came his way, and Parkin, as usual, was as elusive as ever when he did get possession. His opponents looked very feeble indeed.

After the game the players and officials of both clubs attended a dinner at the Grosvenor Hotel where Mr Ernest Parker, one of the Trinity officials, congratulated the Hull club on their 'gem' of a new ground.

He talked about his own playing days for Outwood Church and recalled a game against Hull Kingston Rovers in December 1894 which was played at the Boulevard, Rovers' old ground, before Hull took over the lease.

Mr John Wilson, the secretary of the Rugby League, impressed upon the company that the Northern Union was a thing of the past and the new name of the organisation was the Rugby Football League.

Hull Kingston Rovers ended the season in fourth place and went on to defeat Huddersfield 15–5 in the Championship Final at Headingley. Trinity lost 17 of their 36 games and finished 13th in the league table.

––––––––––

Wakefield Trinity

Pollard, Thompson, Pickup, Siswick, Rosenfield, Rogers, J. Parkin, Agar, Barraclough, Durkin, Gould, Webb, Rafter

Try: Rosenfield

Hull Kingston Rovers

Osborne, Harris, Rees, Cook, Austin, McGiever, McGlone, J.R. Wilkinson, Gibson, Wilkinson, Bielby, Van Rooyen, Westerdale

Attendance: 18,000

Wakefield's superb defence

Yorkshire Challenge Cup second round at Headingley, 14 November 1924

Leeds 4, Wakefield Trinity 5

A dramatic and controversial incident within minutes of the start of the game, coupled with Trinity's tremendous defence, gave Wakefield a famous semi-final victory.

The game was around five minutes old when Wakefield were awarded a penalty; Pollard missed the chance to give Trinity an early lead. The *Yorkshire Post* report of the match described what happened next:

> *Walmsley fielded near the dead ball line. He afterwards threw to Bacon who appeared to cross the dead ball line. The referee ordered a scrummage outside the Leeds goal posts; a decision the accuracy of which raised much discussion.*

The scrum formed and sensing a great chance the Trinity forwards pushed the Leeds pack clean off the ball. Jonty Parkin scooped up the ball, sold the defence a stunning dummy and darted over the line for a try. Pollard converted.

One popular version of the incident suggested that Jonathon Parkin had a suspicion that neither Walmsley nor the ball had left the field of play and actually appealed to the referee to rule for a forward pass by the Leeds full-back.

Wakefield's forwards were in awesome form and behind them Parkin and Pickup took full advantage of an almost endless supply of the ball. The *Yorkshire Post* commented:

There would be many at the match who could recall the Wakefield 'Old Brigade' when the forwards swept all before them by their wonderful grit and determination. Those same characteristics were seen in this struggle. Their policy was to overpower the Leeds forwards, to break up quickly, tackle firmly and effectively and trust to making short dashes for the line.

Although they were beaten in the scrummages the Leeds forwards excelled in loose play and some fine dribbles by Thompson and Davies caused the Wakefield defence several tense moments. One of these strong forward rushes was stopped by Gould, who was then penalised for not playing the ball correctly. Thompson's well-directed kick at goal reduced the lead to just three points. Shortly before half time *'the game developed into excessive robustness'* and after several players had been warned referee Wood sent off Trinity's half-back Pickup for a kicking attack on Binks.

Trinity hastily regrouped: Pollard went to half-back and Glossop withdrew from the pack to the wing. Leeds attacked strongly but Wakefield's defence held out to half-time.

The second half was a keen struggle with some tremendously hard tackling shown by both sides and the referee again had to speak to several players for *'too robust tactics'*.

Leeds were beginning to win more of the ball from the scrums but Parkin's defensive play was outstanding. The *Leeds Mercury* carried this description:

It was in Parkin's spotting of Binks that the half-back exercised his greatest influence on the game. As a matter of fact, Parkin was always near to being offside, but he succeeded in his purpose of preventing Binks from maintaining a service of passes when he did get the ball from the scrum.

Ten minutes from time Jones swooped on to a loose ball and with all avenues to the line blocked he managed to steady himself sufficiently to score a drop goal with a clever left-leg kick.

With just one point separating the sides the final minutes were frantic. Pollard and Batten were temporarily knocked out, then Bacon and Broughton almost scored.

Broughton came close again in the final minute when he followed a kick through over the line only to see *'the cool and calculating Wakefield full-back'* Siswick punt the ball to safety.

It was the final act in a great game. When the referee blew his whistle for time Wakefield Trinity had held on to their unbeaten start to the season with a famous victory.

Across at Hull, Batley maintained their record of never being beaten by Hull Kingston

Siswick, Parkin and Pickup. Jonty Parkin, centre, scored the only try of the game and Pickup, his half-back partner, was sent off by referee Wood for kicking a Leeds player.

Rovers when they held on to a slender two-point lead to defeat the Rovers 10–8 and set up the Final with Wakefield.

Leeds

Walmsley, Broughton, Rosser, Jones, Lyons, Binks, Bacon, Jackson, Grant, Trusler, Thompson, Davies, Thomas

Goals: Thompson, Jones

Wakefield Trinity

Siswick, Pollard, Batten, Reid, Thomas, Parkin, Pickup, Gould, White, Blower, Gibson, Horton, Glossop

Try: Parkin

Goal: Pollard

Attendance: 27,000

Wakefield's sterling scrummages

Yorkshire Challenge Cup Final at Headingley, 22 November 1924
Batley 8, Wakefield Trinity 9

The clash between Trinity and Batley was one of the most eagerly awaited Yorkshire Cup Finals for years. The 'Gallant Youths' of Batley were reigning champions, while Wakefield were unbeaten in 10 games.

Batley, playing with the advantage of a strong wind, rocked Trinity from the kick-off when from the first scrum of the match Kirkby almost scored in the corner. Within a minute a fine round of precision passing gave Davidge the opening to score in the corner. Rees kicked the conversion and Batley were five points in front. Wakefield hit back and:

> *...on the left wing Thomas made a great effort, he first pushed Scott on his back, then he pushed aside Kirkby, and then jumped clean over Robinson, but his progress then ended.*

From a penalty Pollard, *'with a ponderous and judicious kick gained considerable ground.'* Then Glossop, Wakefield's young loose forward *'picked up the ball from the midst of what looked like a crowd of spectators and worked his way through the opposition in a remarkable manner.'*

Jonty Parkin darted forward and in an instant was at Glossop's shoulder, shouting for the ball. Glossop's pass was timed to perfection and Parkin sprinted clean through to touch down under the posts. The Trinity captain converted his own try and the score was level at five-all.

Shortly before half-time Batley's Ike Fowler *'flitted between the heavier and bigger Wakefield men as easily as did Drake's tiny warships slip through the lines of the mighty Armada.'* He slipped the ball to Rees, who scored a superb try near the corner. The conversion was missed,

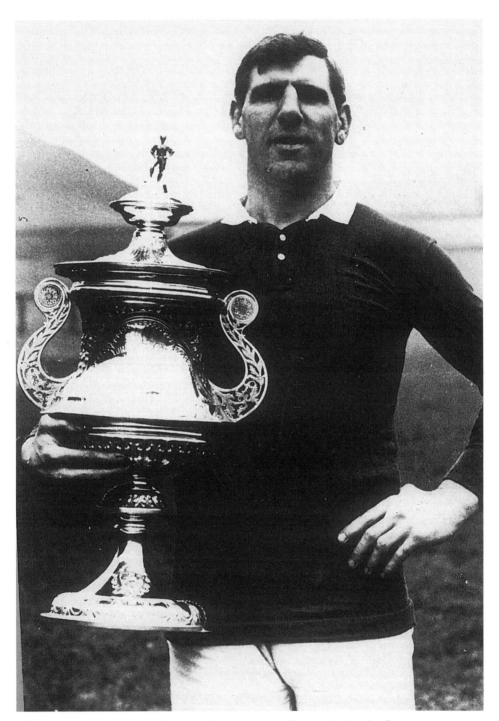

Billy Batten with the Yorkshire Cup. Batten played for Hunslet in the first-ever Yorkshire Cup Final in 1907 when the Parksiders defeated Halifax at Park Avenue, Bradford.

Wakefield's cup-winning team and club officials. Back row: Parker, Sherwood, Gebbard, Jackson, Metcalfe, Brookes, Whiteley, Woodhead. Standing: Quinn, Stocks, White, Abrahams, Blower, Glossop, Horton, Siswick, Crowther. Seated: Bonner, Reid, Pollard, Parkin, Batten, Thomas, Little. In front: Jubb, Pickup.

but Batley went in to the dressing rooms at half-time with a two-point lead.

In the second half Batley embarked upon a series of spoiling tactics that, although designed to win the game, actually cost them the victory. Frank Gallagher obstructed Jonty Parkin and from five yards inside own half Pollard kicked the penalty. Within minutes, and seemingly oblivious to the danger of Pollard's goal-kicking prowess, Batley again obstructed. This time Pollard failed with the kick, but he had little time to wait before Batley obstructed again and this time his kick gave Trinity the one-point lead they had fought for.

Batley were soon playing as a beaten team and with Parkin conjuring up every trick he knew they became even more frustrated. A series of short kicks to touch showed that Wakefield were *'playing for keeps.'*

As a spectacle the game was virtually over. Parkin's spoiling tactics worked well and Wakefield held on to their one-point lead to collect the Yorkshire Challenge Cup for the second time in their history. Jonty Parkin asked a great deal of his team in those closing minutes, 'Yorkist' of the *Leeds Mercury* commenting:

> *Wakefield played a great cup tie game. They never yielded an inch and were always watching for that opportunity, that failure on the part of an opponent, that*

would give them a path to victory. And when it came they struck remorselessly; and then took another deep draught of their boundless fighting spirit to enable them to hold on to what they had gained. It was an abundant flow of this spirit which carried Wakefield to their great achievement.

The Trinity team and officials travelled straight from Headingley to Wakefield in a motor omnibus and were met in the Bull Ring by the Mayor of the City and crowds of their supporters. Following a meal at the Strafford Arms Hotel the players greeted the crowd from the upper windows of the hotel, with captain Jonty Parkin and Billy Batten making short speeches to the crowd. After the formalities were over the team paraded the cup through the streets of Wakefield *'amidst scenes of great enthusiasm.'*

Batley

Robinson, Stacey, Davidge, Rees, Kirkby, Scott, Fowler, Brook, Carter, Douglas, Gallagher, Leeming, Smith

Tries: Davidge, Rees
Goal: Rees

Wakefield Trinity

Abrahams, Pollard, Batten, Reid, Thomas, Parkin, Pickup, Gould, White, Blower, Gibson, Horton, Glossop

Try: Parkin
Goals: Pollard 2, Parkin

Attendance: 25,546

The Parksiders outclassed in all departments

Yorkshire Cup first round replay at Parkside, Hunslet, 17 October 1928

Hunslet 11, Wakefield Trinity 20

In the first round match at Belle Vue, Trinity had fought back from an early set-back to take the lead with around 10 minutes to play. The game seemed to be won until, in the final minute, Hunslet were awarded a penalty and Litt kicked a superb goal to level the match at seven points each.

The replay at Parkside the following Wednesday was a tough game for the Trinitarians. Hunslet's pack, with heavyweights Guerin and Litt to the fore, were a formidable force, and they had caused Wakefield countless problems at Belle Vue. Trinity played the same team as they had at Belle Vue and Hunslet brought in Howarth for Walkington, who had broken his jaw in the first game.

Newspaper headlines trumpet Trinity's achievements.

Glossop, Horton and Pollard. Bill Horton was one of the finest forwards of the era and was capped 14 times for Great Britain.

At Parkside Wakefield were a different team and took the much fancied and confident Hunslet completely by surprise. The *Wakefield Express* commented:

> *The all round improvement in Wakefield's play came as a revelation not only to their own supporters but to those outside people who seemed to think the Trinitarians were rapidly going down the hill.*

One of the features of the match was the brilliant understanding and team work the Wakefield players showed. The forwards were not overawed by the Hunslet pack and this was attributed by observers to the high-quality play of the forwards, who managed to be both masters of the scrummages and alert in loose play.

Trinity took the lead with a Pollard penalty, his only goal of the match, in the 10th minute, and soon afterward scored their first try:

> *The Hunslet backs were getting away with a round of passing when Siswick, observing his opportunity, slipped in and stole one of their passes. Without any hesitation he ran straight away and, on reaching Place, he transferred to Davies, who went over the line.*

Another fine try followed when Bateson chipped the ball over the Hunslet defence and Pearce won the race for the touchdown.

Almost on half-time the Hunslet forwards rushed the ball down the field and Gibson attempted to kick the ball over his own line for safety. The ball took a cruel bounce and Jenkins nipped in for a clever but fortunate try which Litt converted.

In the second half Trinity began *'giving their opponents a very warm time'* and Pollard, following his own towering kick, charged down Guerin's clearance to gather and score a fine opportunist try. Jonty Parkin was now playing a superb game and a pass from '*that box of tricks*' put Davies clear to make ground before passing to Bateson who crossed in the corner.

Wakefield were now playing with the confidence of winners and, as one reporter wrote: '*...their cohesion and quickness completely upset the calculations of Hunslet and several of their movements were clever and attractive.*'

Glossop started a fine movement that completely beat the Hunslet defence, and passed to Bateson who:

> *...confronted by Place, made a movement while on the run, as if attempting to kick.*
> *Place at once turned round in order to make for the line, but Bateson dashed past him*
> *and two other defenders and scored a great try.*

Wakefield scored their final try when Pearce intercepted and passed to Davies to score Trinity's sixth unconverted try.

In the closing stages of the game Smith left the field with an injury, and the Parksiders rallied briefly to score two unconverted tries, but in the end Wakefield had won a fine match by a clear margin.

In the following round Wakefield were dismissed from the competition by Leeds, the eventual winners of the Cup.

Wakefield Trinity

Pollard, Bateson, Davies, Siswick, Smith, Parkin, Pearce, Gibson, Field, Moss, Horton, Maidment, Glossop

Tries: Davies 2, Pearce, Pollard, Bateson 2

Goal: Pollard

Hunslet

Place, Broughton, Howarth, Beverley, Coulson, Young, Thornton, Jenkins, Moss, Traill, Guerin, Litt, Chapman

Tries: Jenkins, Broughton, Howarth

Goal: Litt

Attendance: 8,000

Refused to be beaten

Tour match at Belle Vue, Wakefield, 28 September 1929

Wakefield Trinity 14, Australia 3

When the final whistle had blown at Belle Vue the Australians had been beaten for the first time on the tour and the Wakefield crowd had cheered themselves hoarse. Mr Harry Sunderland, one of the managers of the Australian team, said, *'Well it comes to us all. We are not making any excuses. We've been beaten by a better team on the afternoon.'*

It was a fair statement. Trinity had done their homework on the tourists; they had recognised the dangers posed and developed a strategy to deal with it. They also had a great belief in themselves and, led superbly from the front by Jonathon Parkin, simply refused to be beaten.

The team's results in the lead-up to the meeting could hardly have been more contrasting: the powerful Kangaroos were unbeaten in their first six games, while Trinity had lost four of their first seven league games.

A big feature of the tourists' play in those early tour games had been the speed in which they executed the play of the ball and the ability of their players to hold their arms high when tackled, enabling them to release the ball to colleagues in support.

Trinity snuffed out the threat of these tactics by covering everything that moved in front of them and tackling man and ball and putting them down together. As the game progressed Wakefield improved and tightened their grip on the game. The *Leeds Mercury* commented:

> There came a time when the Australian attack could not move an inch. Trinity's tackling had put them right off the game and men who have been stars in the Australians' previous matches were missing passes, giving passes indifferently and generally showing that they were baffled.

Trinity's defence laid the foundations for the victory but their attacking play was also a

Jonathon 'Jonty' Parkin, Trinity's captain and scourge of many an Australian side. Sharlston-born, Jonty won 17 caps for Great Britain and toured Australia and New Zealand three times, twice as captain of the Lions. He made 342 appearances for Trinity in a career that brought him only one medal, a Yorkshire Cup winners' gong in 1924, in 17 years.

revelation. Directing that attack was the inspirational Jonty Parkin, Trinity's captain, who was no stranger to the Australians or their tactics. Jonty had first toured Australia and New Zealand with the Lions in 1920 before returning as captain in 1924 and 1928.

Parkin's main threat was the Australian Kadwell, the clever little half-back who had played a brilliant game in the 27–5 victory over Batley in the third game of the tour. In only his third match of the season scrum-half Parkin varied his tactics so much he had Kadwell at first puzzled, then completely in his grasp.

Wakefield opened the scoring in the 12th minute, when full-back Pollard kicked a penalty goal. The tourists hit back with a good unconverted try from Finch but within minutes another penalty from Pollard gave Trinity the lead again. Charlie Pollard completed his hat-trick of goals when he cleverly made himself the time and space to drop a goal. Within minutes the ubiquitous Jonty Parkin delivered a gigantic blow to the tourists' already flagging confidence when he intercepted a pass, bluffed the defence and raced under the posts for a try, which Pollard converted to give Trinity an eight-point half-time lead.

The Australians started the second half with a changed line-up following an injury to Maher in the first half. Maher went to full-back, Upton to the wing and Ridley moved to centre. The tourists' forwards made many efforts to get the ball moving in loose play but the Trinity tackling held firm and a subtle change in tactics saw the Trinity forwards rush to the line with the ball at their feet. The *Yorkshire Post* commented:

> *Parkin's tactics behind the scrummage sorely tried the tourists who were persevering with the efforts to pass the ball. They were baffled, however, and there was nothing like the speed and accuracy that they have shown in other games in their work.*

A dribble by Smith took the ball through the Kangaroos' defence; Jones picked up and cleverly transferred to Ray, who raced away from Maher to a score a fine try in the corner.

Pollard missed the conversion attempt. In the final minute Parkin had the chance to increase the winning margin but lost the ball over the line.

Wakefield Trinity

C. Pollard, Ray, Jones, E. Pollard, Smith, Parkin, Davies, Hewitt, White, Higson, Horton, Maidment, Glossop

Tries: Parkin, Ray

Goals: C. Pollard 4

Australia

Upton, Finch, Maher, Fifield, Ridley, Kadwell, Laws, Brogden, Bishop, Root, Kingston, Dempsey, Steinhort

Try: Finch

Attendance: 9,786

Football by floodlight

League game at White City, London, 20 September 1933
London Highfield 8, Wakefield Trinity 9

Ever since the breakaway from the Rugby Football Union in 1895 the Rugby Football League had always attempted to take the 13-a-side code of football to London. New Zealand and Australian touring sides regularly played games in London and in 1929 the League made the innovative and highly successful decision to take the Challenge Cup Final to the Empire Stadium, Wembley.

In 1933 a new attempt to win over the capital came when Brigadier-General A.C. Critchley bought Wigan Highfield and transferred the club from Pemberton to play its home games at White City in the west of London. Critchley was a greyhound racing promoter and saw the advantage of utilising his stadium for midweek rugby league games.

A group of players from the mid-thirties take a rest during a training session. Back row: Moore, Smart, Hobson, Knowles, Exley, Carter, Horton, Appleyard. Front row: Rowan, Herbert, Goodfellow, Field, Wilkinson.

London Highfield began the 1933/34 season with three away games, before entertaining Wakefield Trinity for their first home game, a match played under floodlights.

The Wednesday night match in London attracted a great deal of attention in Wakefield and 250 supporters took advantage of a LNER half-day excursion costing 9/6d to see the game. The train, equipped with the latest buffet restaurant car, left Wakefield Westgate at 1.45 in the afternoon, arrived in London shortly after 5pm and departed from King's Cross at ten past midnight.

Both teams made a good start to the game and it was soon apparent that the match would be a hard one: '...*there was a keenness about the play indicative of the intentions of both sides to give no quarter on this historic occasion.*'

Wakefield had the better of the opening exchanges – '*their forwards were playing a storming game and the backs were not lacking in enterprise*' – but it was Highfield who had the first chance to open the scoring, when from a penalty attempt Belshaw's kick hit the crossbar.

Play fluctuated between the sides until shortly before half-time when '*the vast stadium echoed with applause when Pollard from a penalty kick quite a yard inside his own half sent the ball high and true over the crossbar.*'

Early into the second half Field crashed his way through a line of opponents and set a course straight for the Highfield try line:

> ... *the Highfield full-back was waiting with open arms in a crouching position to receive him, but like a dreadnought Field ran with all his force into Fraser, who did a backward somersault.*

The collision lost Field his momentum and he was overhauled near the line. A quick play the ball to Herberts, who was seemingly '*here there and everywhere*', as one report put it, regained Wakefield the advantage and a swift pass to Pollard saw the centre race over the line for the first try. Pollard missed the conversion but stretched the lead later with a well-struck penalty. From well inside his own half Smart broke away but his corkscrew run was stopped abruptly when Griffin felled the wing man with a '*vicious hook*'. Smart was badly shaken by the tackle and was helped off the field, while Exley was withdrawn from the pack to take his place on the wing.

London bombarded the Trinity line and when the bounce of a loose ball evaded Horton and Pollard, Walker collected well to score a try which Fraser converted.

Trinity gained a little respite from the Highfield attacks when Smart returned to the field, but with his right eye almost closed he was little more than a passenger for the rest of the game.

Wakefield were now reeling from almost constant Highfield pressure and eventually Gordon forced his way over from a scrum. Fraser failed with the conversion but Highfield had a one-point lead.

The final minutes of the match were frantic. Highfield pressed for a try to seal the game and Trinity inched their way forward for a drop-goal attempt. Full-back Bonner failed with one attempt but *'Pollard did the trick shortly afterwards when he enhanced his goal kicking reputation with a beautiful shot from near the halfway line.'*

Highfield threw everything into attack but Trinity's courageous defence held and Wakefield were the first victors at London Highfield's White City stadium.

London Highfield

Fraser, Walker, Belshaw, Hunter, Maloney, Gordon, Haigh, Hitchen, Fairhurst, Woods, Gray, Griffen, Collier

Tries: Walker, Gordon

Goal: Fraser

Wakefield Trinity

Bonner, Brogden, Farrar, Pollard, Smart, Pearce, Herberts, Higson, Field, Hobson, Horton, Exley, Wilkinson

Try: Pollard

Goals: Pollard 3

Attendance: 5,000

Leeds and Wakefield to meet for the third time

Yorkshire Challenge Cup Final second replay at Fartown,
Huddersfield,
31 October 1934

Leeds 2, Wakefield Trinity 2

A huge crowd of 22,598 assembled at Dewsbury's Crown Flatt ground for the eagerly anticipated Yorkshire Cup Final between Wakefield and Leeds. Trinity's supporters had travelled from Kirkgate and Westgate railway stations and in addition to the normal service, a fleet of 27 buses, each with 32 passengers, left the Market Ground at intervals.

Any thoughts of a fine open game were dismissed with a gale-force wind driving rain straight down the ground's notorious slope. Trinity won the toss and used the wind and the slope to take the lead from a fine try by Burrows, which Pollard converted. In the second half Jubb snapped up a loose ball when half-backs Burrows and Pickup collided with each other and scored a great opportunist try. Brough landed a superb goal to square the game at five points all.

The following Wednesday the teams met again at Huddersfield's Fartown ground for a game that never really started until the final 10 minutes. The *Yorkshire Post* commented:

> *There were 10,500 spectators here this afternoon, when we were reminded in no uncertain fashion of the nearness of winter – there was snow on the hills overlooking the ground – and would reckon, as we did, that the replay was made worth while by its last ten minutes.*

Trinity's team for the game at Fartown. Standing: Moore, Farrar, Hobson, Horton, Smith, Exley, Smart, Bonner. Front: Pollard, Burrows, Field, Wilkinson, Rowan.

The first half was a hectic scramble during which neither side launched '*a back movement that calls for mention*'. Wakefield took a two-point lead in the first half when Pollard kicked a fine penalty goal.

The first 30 minutes of the second half were memorable if only for the countless faults both sides made. Passes constantly went astray and the ball was dropped and knocked on with an alarming frequency. Then Leeds, facing defeat, found their hands, their feet and their form:

> *They realised that they had a three-quarter line in which there are three of the*
> *fastest men in the league; the men in that three-quarter line, at last, understood*
> *that they had a chance if they threw the ball about; and, with the Wakefield heroes*
> *– Exley, Horton, Pollard, Smith and the others – fighting with glorious resolution*
> *to save their line, the struggle became a magnificent affair.*

Leeds tried everything: they whipped the ball across the line to the wing and then back inside again, kicked short through the Wakefield line, and their forwards began to break clean at last at the scrums. A superb kick-through by Busch brought a try-saving run from Horton, '*who pounded along with such men as Harris, Brogden and Smith striving to beat him. Horton flung himself on the ball with the line a yard away.*'

The Loiners had allowed Trinity to say which course the game should take from the start and their forwards had failed to set up important and immediate counter-attacks. They lacked faith in themselves and it took too long for them to realise that they could not beat Trinity at Trinity's game.

Wakefield's forwards played a magnificent match:

> *Rowan, Horton, Hobson and Exley were tireless workers. Exley's ranging of the field in defence in the second half was only equalled by that of Ernest Pollard, who must have left Brogden with the impression that in the course of the game he had acquired another shadow.*

In the final minute of the game Trinity were forced to drop out from their try line, but instead of kicking towards the touch line, the ball sailed straight to Ralph, who, from a perfect position in the centre of the pitch, calmly dropped a goal to give Leeds a draw.

A week later the teams met again at Parkside, Hunslet and, watched by a crowd of 19,304, Leeds defeated Wakefield 13–0, with Stanley Smith, the Fitzwilliam-born former Trinity player, scoring a hat-trick of tries.

————

Leeds

Brough, Harris, Brogden, Parker, Smith, Ralph, Busch, Higson, Lowe, Satterthwaite, Jubb, Dyer, Aspinall

Goal: Ralph

Wakefield Trinity

Bonner, Farrar, Smith, Moore, Smart, Pollard, Burrows, Wilkinson, Field, Hobson, Horton, Exley, Rowan

Goal: Pollard

Attendance: 10,500

Let 'em all come!

Challenge Cup third round at Belle Vue, 13 March 1937
Wakefield Trinity 5, Warrington 0

Wakefield's quest for the 1937 Challenge Cup began with a superb victory over the Cup-holders Leeds and then a hard-fought win over Halifax at Thrum Hall.

On the Thursday before the game the city was covered with a huge fall of snow. Belle Vue was blanketed in snow and with more forecast club chairman A.A. Bonner took the brave decision, the day before the match, to engage a host of men to clear the pitch and terraces. Further anticipated snow held off but even with the ground in good condition Saturday brought more problems for the Wakefield committee. The *Wakefield Express* describes the scene at Belle Vue:

> *There was a time on Saturday when it looked as if the match would not take place. Darkness covered the town, and when the match started, so bad was the light, that it was impossible to see the people on the other side of the field. Eventually, however, the darkness disappeared, and it was possible to follow the game with reasonable comfort.*

Trinity received a huge blow to their confidence when they received a telegram from the team captain Bill Horton, who was delayed in Bristol on business. Horton, the pack leader, was in the process of buying a hotel near Weston-super-Mare and the news of his absence was a great disappointment to the Wakefield crowd. His place was taken by Eddoms.

Warrington were missing their full-back Holden, but his place was taken by Jones, *'a youngster who sailed triumphantly through his first senior Rugby League game with the coolness of a veteran'*.

From the kick-off it was soon obvious that the heavy, muddy ground was hardly likely to allow a spectacular game, and it was clear that the forwards would have to bear the brunt of the battle.

Trinity's players and their followers knew full well that they faced one of the firm favourites to win the Challenge Cup, and one of the fiercest packs of forwards in the Rugby Football League. Warrington's front row were well known for their 'vigorous' methods.

Warrington, with Arkwright and Miller leading from the front, started the game with a series of strong forward movements, tearing into the Wakefield defence *'in a manner which seemed to suggest that they had made up their minds that they were the people who were going to boss the show'*.

A caricatured account of the Trinity v Warrington game.

From the outset, and led magnificently by Mick Exley, the Trinity six never flinched and the way that they maintained their momentum throughout the match was a tribute to their fitness.

Although the forward battle was being gradually won by Trinity, Warrington's brilliant half-back combination of Goodhall and De Lloyd troubled the Wakefield defence throughout the first half.

In the second half, wily scrum-half Goodfellow realised that Warrington were far from happy defending forward rushes and he began to launch his tireless forwards in sweeping dribbling moves that were soon threatening the Wire-pullers' line.

Warrington were still capable of launching their own assaults and from one of these moves the ball ran loose. Watson, Trinity's young loose forward, scooped up the ball and in the words of the *Wakefield Express* reporter:

> *... strode past three or four opponents, and then gave a perfect pass to Malpass. The latter transferred to Milner, who when challenged, put in a cross kick, and Malpass, following up quickly, started a dribble. Near the line the ball squirted towards Herbert, who completed the movement which Milner converted.*

It was a magnificent move that had covered three-quarters of the field and gave Trinity almost complete command. Warrington's fearsome forwards had been overcome and beaten at their own game:

> *... in the loose the Warrington forwards were unable to stay the pace, and even before they showed signs of tiredness they were no match for the Trinitarians who moved fast and acted quickly and rendered valuable assistance to their backs when any tackling had to be done.*

Wakefield drew Keighley in the semi-final and, following a drab 0–0 game, witnessed by 39,998 at Headingley, they lost the replay, and the chance to play at Wembley, by three points to five at Fartown, Huddersfield.

Wakefield Trinity

Teall, Milner, Malpass, Whitworth, Appleyard, Goodfellow, Herbert, Wilkinson, Carter, Eddom, Exley, Flowers, Watson

Try: Herbert
Goal: Milner

Warrington

Jones, Brown, Dingsdale, Shankland, Jenkins, Goodhall, De Lloyd, Rankin, Coton, Miller, Arkwright, Chadwick, Welsby

Attendance: 22,075

Thrills galore at Belle Vue

League match at Belle Vue, 28 December 1937
Wakefield Trinity 5, Hunslet 5

Trinity's third game in four days was described by the *Wakefield Express* as '*one of the most thrilling and interesting seen on this famous ground for a very long time.*'

Wakefield were without Herbert Goodfellow and played the young, inexperienced Ball in his place. Eric Batten was missing from the Hunslet side and his place on the right wing was taken by Jenner, who was a local boy with a considerable aptitude for the game.

The game was dominated by the two packs of forwards, with Hunslet having the slight edge in the scrums, but Trinity's six excelling in loose play. As the report said, '*they were quick and decisive in open play and covered the field like a blanket to beat Hunslet's attacking plans.*'

The first half developed into a very evenly matched 40 minutes, and with defences on top throughout, both teams were denied the chance to create any real opportunities.

Hunslet's young wing man Jenner '*got clear away, but to the relief of Trinity and the obvious disappointment of Hunslet, Teall whipped across and stopped his career a few yards from the line.*'

Wakefield were awarded a penalty and Lee, with a poor kick from a good position, failed to give Trinity the lead. Twice after this Hunslet were penalised but the points on offer were squandered when both kicks were sent to touch to try and gain a foothold in the Hunslet half.

Trinity's stand-off Jones gradually began to cause the Hunslet defence huge problems, with a clever mixture of long and short kicks and the occasional darting run from behind the scrum. Shortly before half-time Jones scooped the ball from a scrum and swept for the line, only to throw out a forward pass when a try looked certain.

Wakefield made several changes for the start of the second half. Ball, who had had a torrid

Harry Wilkinson's giant frame is well captured in this caricature.

time opposing the vastly experienced Thornton, went to the wing. Whitworth moved to centre and Jones to scrum-half.

Ten minutes into the second half Wakefield full-back Teall gathered the ball from a Hunslet kick and *'raced past several opponents and passed to Eddom. The latter at once transferred to Wilkinson, who crossed over the line under the posts for Lee to kick the goal.'* It was the breakthrough Trinity had searched long and hard for, and with a five-point lead they relaxed a little. Wakefield were attacking close to the Hunslet line when a sloppy pass gave Winter the chance to dart into the Trinity line and intercept. Full-back Teall had deserted his position to link into the line and Winter had a clear field in front of him, as the ex-Featherstone centre *'ran for over three parts the length of the field to score a try, which Walkington had no difficulty in converting.'*

Lee had yet another unsuccessful shot at goal for Trinity and then an intense period of Hunslet attacking broke down with an attempted drop at goal.

Wakefield rallied and from a difficult angle Teall failed with an optimistic drop goal attempt. The Parksiders threw everything forward in the final 10 minutes, but time after time mistakes were made and Trinity, in characteristic fashion, took full advantage of the lack of accuracy of their opponents.

In a moment of drama shortly before the final whistle Hunslet's Irish wing man O'Sullivan *'got away and a try seemed certain, but Whitworth ran across from the opposite wing and brought his man down when two or three strides would have taken him over the line.'* It was the final act in a breathtaking game, on which The *Yorkshire Post* commented:

It was only right that the match should end in a draw, for when everything was taken into consideration the side were as evenly matched as they could be. Trinity will perhaps argue that they were unlucky that Lee was out of form in his goal kicking, but on the other hand they were saved more than once by handling faults on the part of the faster Hunslet backs.

Hunslet went on to defeat Leeds in the Championship Final at Elland Road, Leeds, and Trinity ended the season in a tenth place with 21 wins from 36 games.

———————

Wakefield Trinity

Teall, Whitworth, Turner, Malpass, Ryan, Ball, Jones, Wilkinson, Lee, Eddom, Exley, Flowers, Bratley

Try: Wilkinson

Goal: Lee

Hunslet

Walkington, Jenner, Morrell, O'Sullivan, Thornton, Morris, Britton, White, Bennett, Tiffany, Newbound, Stansfield

Try: Winter

Goal: Walkington

Attendance: 5,000

Stott's dramatic goal

Challenge Cup Final at Wembley, 4 May 1946
Wakefield 13, Wigan 12

The first Final to be played at Wembley since the end of World War Two produced a game which was:

> *...exciting rather than skilful and mistakes were often made by both teams, who in the hope of gaining an extra yard made wild and ill directed passes when a little thought would have produced scoring chances.*

The hastily arranged British Lions tour to Australasia had left both sides missing key players for the Wembley Final. Trinity were without Harry Murphy and Wigan lacked Martin Ryan, Joe Egan, Ken Gee and Ted Ward.

Wigan started well, with their forwards holding Wakefield in the loose and gaining good possession from the scrums. Seven minutes into the game J. Blan scored Wigan's opening try following a marvellous forward rush down the centre of the field. Nordgren failed with the conversion attempt.

Wakefield were struggling and finding it very difficult to halt the quick-moving Wigan side. On 20 minutes the Wigan three-quarters Ratcliffe and Ashcroft carved open the Trinity defence with a superb break. The ball was quickly transferred to Nordgren and the New Zealand wing man sped half the length of the field to go over for a try in the corner.

Wakefield finally gained some composure, and when Rylance slipped a superb pass to Stott, *'he scored his side's first try by varying his step cleverly and, using an adroit side-step beat three men to in very little space before going over in the corner.'* Stott missed the kick, but 10 minutes later landed a penalty to put Trinity within a point of Wigan.

Early in the second half, one of a series of Wakefield forays into the Wigan half ended when the ball spun loose from Stott's grasp following a careless pass. Stan Jolley, the Wigan wing

The official programme for the Cup Final at Wembley.

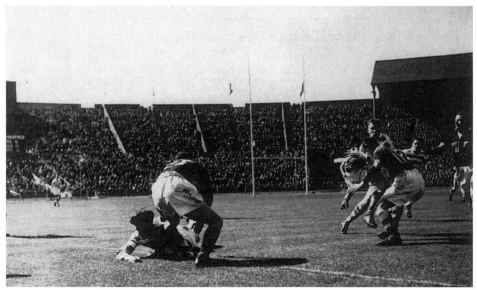

The Trinity defence scramble to foil another dangerous Wigan attack.

man, pounced on the ball and sprinted 70 yards for a try. Again Nordgren failed to add the extra two points with a poor kick.

Trinity rallied again and Goodfellow sliced open a huge gap and passed to Stott, who ran over unopposed for a try, which he failed to convert.

Nordgren crossed for his second try in a move which was thought to be the brightest of the match.

> *Cunliffe, during a long kicking duel, suddenly made his mind up to run and dodging and swerving almost reached the line before being pulled up. From the resultant mix up Nordgren scored.*

The normally sure goal-kicker once again failed to convert, but, with 10 minutes remaining and four points in front the Cup looked destined for Wigan. Wakefield needed something special and it came from their Wigan-born centre, Jim Croston:

> *Croston, a little slower than of old, using his head to save his feet, found a gap in the Wigan defence and, with craft and guile, ran in for a try when the defence was expecting him to pass.*

The Trinity players keep a close eye on Wigan's Nordgren as he sends the ball wide of the posts.

The victorious team parade the cup around the city on a dray loaned by local brewers Beverley Brothers.

The abysmal exhibition of goal-kicking continued when Stott missed the conversion which would have given Trinity a one-point lead.

With around 90 seconds of play left Wigan amazingly conceded a penalty with a blatant obstruction. Stott did his best to compose himself and from a position around 10 yards in from the touch line and almost on the Wigan 25-yard line, his left foot sent the ball in a perfect arc straight through the uprights. With his last kick of the match Stott had given Trinity the lead for the first time and the Challenge Cup was on its way back to Wakefield for the first time since the 'Dreadnoughts' of 1909 triumphed at Headingley.

Oldham-born Stott's overall performance in the Final earned him the very first Lance Todd Trophy for 'Man of the Match'. The *Guardian* wrote of Stott:

> ...*he played as a captain should, foraging splendidly, supporting his half-backs in good attacking moves, and with Croston he was the rock on which many of Wigan's schemes were dashed.*

Wakefield Trinity

Teall, Rylance, Stott, Croston, Baddeley, Jones, Goodfellow, Wilkinson, Marston, Higgins, Exley, Howes, Bratley

Tries: Stott 2, Croston

Goals: Stott 2

Wigan

Cunliffe, Nordgren, Ratcliffe, Ashcroft, Jolley, Lowry, Bradshaw, Banks, J. Blan, Barton, Watkins, Atkinson, W. Blan

Tries: Nordgren 2, Jolley, J. Blan

Attendance: 54,730

Trinity keep Cup promise

Yorkshire Cup Final at Headingley, Leeds, 2 November 1946
Hull 0, Wakefield Trinity 10

Wakefield Trinity kept a year-old promise when they defeated a strong Hull side to win the Yorkshire Challenge Cup for the first time since 1924.

A single defensive slip in the 1945 final against Bradford Northern at Thrum Hall had cost Trinity the Yorkshire Cup. After the match Jim Croston, Wakefield's captain on the day, told the disappointed Trinity supporters that if they got another chance to win the Cup there would be no mistakes.

Wakefield began the Cup trail at Keighley, where they lost 11–14 in the first leg, but defeated the Lawkholmers 8–2 in the return at Belle Vue. Castleford were defeated 11–2 in the

Wakefield's defence slides across to cover a Hull kick to the line.

Trinity's wing man Baddeley attempts to race clear of the Hull defence.

second round at Belle Vue and a strong Hunslet side were beaten 7–4 in a tough and highly controversial semi-final.

Hull's route to the final saw victories over Featherstone Rovers, York, and a stirring 15–11 defeat of cross-city rivals Hull Kingston Rovers in the semi-final at the Boulevard.

Trinity knew full well the powers of the awesome Hull pack, with the *Yorkshire Post* commenting:

> *Trinity at full strength could never claim an advantage forward either in the scrummage or in the loose, but it is a tribute to them that they did not allow the strong Hull pack to subdue them.*

The first half was a very open game and although defences were always far better than any of the attacking movements, both sides '*showed enterprise and a willingness to keep the ball on the move.*'

In the first 20 minutes Hull looked the more dangerous and seemed likely to take a firm grip on the game. The Wakefield players held firm and gradually began to assert themselves more in attack.

Johnson, the Hull scrum half, constantly probed the Wakefield defence when he shrewdly kicked the ball through for his alert wing men Bowers and Glynn. His middle backs let him down somewhat, when all the moves they could muster were to run straight, in the hope that the Trinity defence would make mistakes. Trinity were not in the mood to make mistakes, and their defence held firm throughout the half.

Three minutes into the second half Trinity struck a massive blow to Hull:

> *Wilkinson's pass from a ruck in the corner caught the Hull defence a yard out of*

position, and although Fletcher was held under the posts Croston cannoned into him and his tacklers from behind and the try was made.

Perry kicked the conversion but Trinity had paid a high price for the three-point lead. Fletcher had sprained his ankle in the act of scoring and took no further part in the game.

Trinity's second try came from more quick-thinking from the ever-alert Croston:

When Rylance passed to him and then raced behind him for the return, Croston allowed the Hull defence to concentrate on Rylance and then, turning completely round, drove straight down the middle himself to confuse the defence and eventually send Rylance over.

It was a superb move, a brilliant try and it instantly sealed Hull's fate.

Wakefield, with a 10-point lead and down to 12 men, adopted a policy of maintaining their advantage rather than going all-out to increase it. Hull tried and tried to break through, but Trinity's courage and teamwork in defence were just as efficient with a man short as they had been in the first half.

The huge crowd generated receipts of £3,720. Wakefield and Hull were each to receive £800, but Bramley were awarded a third of Trinity's share as compensation for the loss of their home fixture against Wakefield. Hunslet were also given compensation as the crowd at Headingley reduced the attendance for their home game against Hull Kingston Rovers.

Wakefield Trinity

Teall, Perry, Jones, Croston, Baddeley, Rylance, Fletcher, Wilkinson, Marson, Higgins, Exley, Murphy, Bratley

Tries: Rylance, Fletcher

Goals: Perry 2

Hull

Miller, Glynn, Watts, Sinclair, Bowers, Lawrence, Johnson, Shillito, Wilkinson, Jimmison, Booth, Tindall, Shakesby

Attendance: 29,000

Trinity's revenge

League match at Belle Vue, 4 January 1947
Wakefield Trinity 8, Wigan 7

Wakefield gained revenge for their New Year's Day defeat at Central Park with a dramatic victory in a rousing game.

Both teams were severely weakened. Wigan had Gee, Egan, Ryan, Ashcroft and Bradshaw all absent on county duty and Trinity, already hard hit by injuries, were further weakened with the withdrawal of Wilkinson.

Before the kick-off both sides were photographed with the magnificent array of silverware they had won the previous season.

A heavy Belle Vue pitch favoured the forwards and as the game wore on it became apparent that Trinity's set of six were playing a wonderful game. The *Wakefield Express* commented:

> *The Wakefield forwards were masters in both the scrummages and loose work. None worked harder than Booth and Howes. The front row man confirmed earlier opinion that his usefulness in open field work on top of his work in the scrums, must soon win for him a permanent place in the side.*

From the kick-off Wakefield made good use of the strong wind that blew down the ground and were soon pressing the Wigan lines. Full-back Teall fielded a kick well and gained good ground before transferring to Longley; the centre passed swiftly to Stott, who gave Perry a good opening. Wigan's defence moved to cover the danger on the wing but Perry launched a superb cross kick straight to Brooks, who crossed the line but failed to ground the ball correctly. Ten minutes later Banks passed to Brooks, who fooled Wigan with a neat little inside pass to Bratley, who crashed over the line from 10 yards out. Stott converted the try with a wonderful, towering kick from near the touchline.

Wakefield and Wigan line up with their haul of trophies. The Trinity players are, back row: Baddeley, Higgins, Exley, Longley, Marson, Booth, Howes, Bratley. Front: Brooks, Banks, Perry, Stott, Wilkinson, Teall.

Shortly before the break Wigan were weakened when Ratcliffe broke a bone in his ankle.

Early in the second half Ward kicked a penalty goal for Wigan but the Wakefield half-backs were having a superb game. The *Wakefield Express* commented:

> *It speaks well for the Trinity defence that neither Mountford, Ward, nor Lawrenson found a loophole from near the scrums. At half-back the Wakefield pair were up against tough opposition but neither Banks nor Brooks gave anything away. With a good supply of the ball Banks opened out very well, although some of his punts to ward off the close spotting of Wigan were badly directed.*

Wakefield were coasting to a famous victory when five minutes from time Wigan were awarded a penalty and:

> *Ward put the ball high into the air to allow the wind to supply all the motive power possible. As the ball sailed gracefully earthwards, Nordgren was there to receive it and touch down for a try.*

Ward stunned the crowd with his conversion and with minutes remaining Wigan were two points in front. Wakefield, however, were not to be subdued and *'working their way into the Wigan half, Banks emerged from a bunch of players and darted over for a try – a match winner.'*

Stott failed with the kick but from the restart kick-off the referee blew for time. Trinity's followers went wild with a mixture of delight, relief and disbelief.

Following the game the players and officials from both clubs were entertained to tea at the Town Hall, where Mr L. Jackson, the Trinity Chairman, congratulated both clubs on their fine achievement in winning three trophies each.

It was announced at the tea that the photographs of the teams and trophies that had been taken that afternoon were to be sold to aid the benefit of Harry Wilkinson, the great Trinity forward.

Wigan were crowned Champions at the end of the season, beating Dewsbury 14–4 in the Final at Maine Road, Manchester. Trinity finished 10th in the table, winning 20 of their 36 games.

––––––––––

Wakefield Trinity

Teall, Perry, Stott, Longley, Baddeley, Brooks, Banks, Booth, Marson, Higgins, Exley, Howes, Bratley

Try: Bratley, Banks

Goals: Stott

Wigan

Cunliffe, Ratcliffe, Ward, Lawrenson, Nordgren, Mountford, Toohey, Woosey, Shovanton, Banks, Atkinson, W. Blan, J. Blan

Try: Nordgren

Goals: Ward 2

Attendance: 11,000

Trinity win the Yorkshire Cup again

Yorkshire Challenge Cup Final replay at Odsal Stadium, Bradford,
5 November 1947

Leeds 7, Wakefield Trinity 8

Leeds and Wakefield drew the first Yorkshire Cup Final 7–7 in a gruelling and tough encounter at Fartown. Trinity had taken a first-half lead with a goal from Stott and then scored a fine try when, *'In a typical Goodfellow "blinder" the scrum half took a pass from Marson, and sailed in between two defenders for a try under the posts.'*

Stott converted the try and later kicked a penalty goal.

Whitehead kicked a penalty for Leeds and then, with around 10 minutes to play, they scored an amazing try to level the game. Stott took a penalty attempt and although Kelly did not take the ball cleanly and there were appeals for a knock-on, play proceeded over a distance of about 70 yards of brilliant passing and re-passing in which Williams, Cook, Price and Warrior figured. They finished with a try when Williams grounded the ball behind the Wakefield posts. The *Wakefield Express* commented:

> *There is no desire to rub salt into the wound, but one cannot refrain from expressing astonishment at seeing Trinity players who could have stopped Williams planting the ball in such an easy position for a goal kick halt in their striding to appeal for a forward pass.*

Both clubs made changes for the replay at Odsal. Stott stepped down with an injured knee and Rylance took his place. Rylance's inclusion was a surprise to the Wakefield followers as he had withdrawn from the England team to face France with a groin injury and was expected to

CUP FINAL REPLAY

WAKEFIELD
TRINITY

LEEDS

Wednesday, Nov. 5th, 1947

KICK-OFF 3-0 p.m.

**OFFICIAL
PROGRAMME** 3**D.**

Ron Rylance collects the Yorkshire Challenge Cup.

be out for a month. Brereton took the place of Whitehead in the Leeds pack.

An unusually quiet first half saw Trinity take the lead with a penalty goal from Perry.

Leeds opened the second-half scoring when New Zealander Bert Cook dropped a fine goal. Trinity pressed hard and after squandering several scoring chances Wilkinson finally crossed the Loiners' line. Leeds lost their rhythm and composure in defence and a dropped pass gave Bratley the opportunity to scoop up the ball and score a try, which Perry failed to convert.

A dreadful blunder by Wakefield gave Flanagan an easy try, which Whitehead converted to bring Leeds with a point of Trinity. They came to life immediately and, as the *Wakefield Express* commented:

> *With the score at 8–7 the tense atmosphere can be better imagined than described.*
> *On every kick, every pass, aye, every movement on the field eyes were focused and*
> *it was a relief, even though Trinity had recovered their normal composure, when*
> *the whistle called an end to the proceedings.*

Wakefield's victory was the result of a good, solid performance, which was dominated by their veteran forwards Wilkinson, Murphy, Booth and Bratley. Their defence in the face of a Leeds side that used a variety of clever back passes to try and create openings never faltered and although the clever pairing of Williams and Jenkins did bluff Trinity for the two tries they were never split wide open.

Wakefield Trinity

Teall, Perry, Jenkinson, Boocker, Rylance, Fletcher, Goodfellow, Wilkinson, Marson, Higgins, Murphy, Booth, Bratley

Tries: Bratley, Wilkinson

Goal: Perry

Leeds

Kelly, Warrior, Cook, Price, Whitehead, Williams, Jenkins, Prosser, Carter, Brereton, Clues, Flanagan, Owens

Try: Flanagan

Goals: Cook, Whitehead

Attendance: 32,500

Trinity's superb forwards

Yorkshire Challenge Cup Final at Fartown, Huddersfield,
27 October 1951

Keighley 3, Wakefield Trinity 17

Trinity began their Yorkshire Cup campaign with a tricky two-legged first round draw with Hull. They defeated the Airlie Birds 15–5 at Belle Vue and held on to draw 18-all at the Boulevard.

In the second round they defeated cup-holders Huddersfield 14–5 at Belle Vue. Then, in a thrilling semi-final at Headingley, Trinity's magnificent defence held on under almost constant pressure to beat Leeds by a single point.

Keighley had overcome Castleford and Halifax and in the semi-final defeated Hunslet 15–9.

It was Trinity's 10th Yorkshire Cup Final and Keighley's second, having lost to Bradford Northern in the two-legged 1943 Final.

Keighley began the match with a fine display from their work-hungry pack of forwards, with Brereton playing a real captain's game at the front.

Wakefield's forwards were well prepared for the onslaught and, as the *Wakefield Express* commented:

> *Wakefield's forte was the forward department. There, Keighley faced a set of Tartars whose stranglehold never relaxed and the effect of which was so obvious long before the end as the drooping figures of certain Keighley forwards testified.*

Leading the Trinity forwards was the veteran Bill Hudson, who '*roamed the field striking apprehension into the hearts of any opponent within reach.*'

Yorkshire Cup for Trinity

Worthy conquerors of Keighley

FOR the third time since the war, Wakefield Trinity have won the Yorkshire Cup. At Huddersfield, last Saturday, they were worthy winners over Keighley, who were making their first peace-time appearance in the county cup final and who have, never in their history, had the pleasure of winning the trophy.

The game never reached a classical standard, and to non-partisans it would admittedly not be a very entertaining affair. But that is not to say the game was without its bright moments. It was a match which merited a better label than "typical cup-tie," for students of Rugby League would observe in this set-to tactical skill in generous proportions as first one and then another piece of adroit planning had to be scrapped to meet changing circumstances.

Wakefield T. (4 goals, 3 tries) ... 17 points

Keighley (1 try) .... 3 points

There was no "Lance Todd" trophy awarded for the outstanding individual in this game. If there had been, to whom would it have gone?

Allowing a little sentiment to creep into our judgment, we suggest that before an award for such distinguished service was decided, the name of "Bill" Hudson would have merited consideration.

Whilst the mere presence on the field of the veteran Wakefield skipper was of a value difficult to assess on the basis of its worth from an inspirational standpoint, its intrinsic value was there for all to see as he roamed the field striking apprehension into the hearts of any opponent within reach!

"Bill," of the wisp of golden hair, has got his long-cherished Yorkshire Cup medal! And how appropriate it was that he should earn it—yes, *earn* is the word — with Wakefield Trinity, a team with which he might easily have spent his best days instead of his declining years. Declining, did we say? Not on Saturday's showing!

However, to permit stern reality

wall" position in which Wakefield found themselves, the scene was changed to one of assault by the judicious use of a penalty kick by Meredith. He punted the ball nearly three-parts the length of the field to find touch behind the Keighley "25" line. And here, one of those odd tricks of fate gave Wakefield the ball from a scrum—the second time out of only four in the entire first half! But surprise at seeing the ball emerge on the Wakefield side of the pack was overshadowed by the surprise to follow when Fletcher shot away rather wide from the scrum and suddenly turned to send the ball inside to Hughes, who went over the Keighley line through a gap left open in astounding fashion. Not one of the three rear Keighley forwards was there in time to shake Hughes by the neck—or hand.

The position was such that Hirst simply could not miss with the goal kick, and there was little wonder that, at long range, our interpretation—by lip reading—of captain Brereton's remarks to his men seemed to indicate that he was not very pleased with them!

Newspaper cutting describing the match action.

Keighley monopolised the first-half scrums, heeling the ball from 14 of the 18 set pieces, but the possession gained was often wasted. They constantly attempted to batter their way through the Trinity defence with a series of vigorous rushes.

Trinity's breakthrough came early in the first half when, against the run of play, they won the ball from a scrum on the Keighley 25-yard line, and Fletcher snatched the ball and ran wide from the scrum before turning to pass the ball back inside to loose forward Hughes.

The Keighley back three forwards had all followed Fletcher's wide run and had left a huge gap, into which Hughes raced, completely unchallenged, to score a try that Hirst converted with ease.

In the second half Hirst extended Wakefield's lead to 9–3 with two penalty goals and, with the game slipping away from them, Keighley's forwards began to tire.

Keighley were now a jaded side and the power and thrust of their forwards, which had given them so much of the ball in the first half, had gone. Trinity began to win far more of the ball from the scrums and half-backs Fletcher and Meredith began to use the ball well.

With around 10 minutes left to play Trinity hurled everything they had at the Keighley line, and Hughes and Booth were denied certain tries before Don Robinson struck with a superb try.

Jack Booth captured in a superb caricature.

The *Wakefield Express* reported:

Finally Robinson, from about ten yards' distance, showed how he could compress his huge and strong frame through the metaphorical eye of a needle. His was an amazing gallop in restricted space to beat four defenders before finally diving over the line.

The try, from the 19-year-old iron foundry apprentice, crowned a brilliant individual performance in his very first Cup Final.

In the final minute of the game the Wakefield backs opened out in grand style, and one of the slickest and fastest rounds of passing of the game gave Welsh international wing man Booker a richly deserved try in the corner.

After the match the Trinity players and officials returned to Wakefield for a celebratory dinner at the Strafford Arms Hotel.

Wakefield Trinity

Luckman, Duggan, Hirst, Froggatt, Booker, Meredith, Fletcher, Booth, Horner, Hudson, Howes, Robinson, Hughes

Tries: Booker, Robinson, Hughes

Goals: Hirst 4

Keighley

Lockwood, Ward, Taylor, Creeney, Ivill, Redman, Barratt, Brereton, Britton, Ramsden, Mulhall, Kelly, Sanderson

Try: Redman

Attendance: 25,495

Two tries and a medal in his first Cup Final

Yorkshire Challenge Cup Final at Headingley, Leeds, 20 October 1956

Hunslet 5, Wakefield Trinity 23

At the end of a rousing Yorkshire Cup Final at Headingley two players epitomised the highs and lows of Rugby League Football.

On the Hunslet side was Australian forward Arthur Clues, a veteran of 70 cup ties, all bumps, bruises and weariness, and without a single winner's medal. On the Wakefield side stood 20-year-old Fred Smith, all smiles and sprightliness, thinking how wonderful it was to play in your very first cup tie and win a gold medal.

Fred Smith, whom Trinity had signed from Leeds, certainly deserved his medal: he scored the first two tries and was rock solid in defence.

Trinity's victory lay in the fact that they were lighter and faster in both attack and defence than their opponents. As one report commented: *'what Trinity's forwards lost on the scales they made up on the running track. They moved the ball about quicker than their heavier opponents.'*

Trinity opened the scoring seven minutes into the game when Holliday broke through the Hunslet defence and ran straight down the centre of the pitch. He sensed the danger of the Parksiders' cover moving quickly across to cover the wing and, with a superb long pass, missed out Albert Mortimer and transferred to Smith, who scored in the corner. Frank Mortimer kicked the conversion and then landed a penalty before Hunslet opened their scoring with a penalty from Talbot.

In the 26th minute Fred Smith scored his second try when:

> *A pass from Armstead dispatched the young Mortimer on his journey, and, not for the only time in the game, he beat his opposite number with a neat side step and*

retained possession long enough to require full-back Langton's attention before sending on to Smith. The winger was away like a flash to plant the ball over the line with barely shoulder room between the touch down spot and the corner flag.

Hunslet hit back and hit back hard, their colossal forwards pounding away at the Trinity defences in wave after wave of terrifically powerful onslaughts. Trinity held firm and even when their line was breached, they found they had the pace to streak back to tackle almost certain try-scoring breaks.

Shortly before half-time Child eventually scored for Hunslet.

On the hour Trinity sealed the game with a 10 points in two minutes scoring spree that rocked Hunslet. The first try came when:

...centre Mortimer took advantage of a loose ball dropped by Arthur Clues and dribbled it out of the reach of two defenders before finally beating Waite in following a fly kick towards the line.

Two minutes later a good break from Holliday put Chamberlain through and, while being

Trinity, the Yorkshire Challenge Cup winners of 1956. Back row: McGee, Thomas, Froggett, West, Hadfield, Simpson, Sugden, Wilkinson. Seated: Bell, Mortimer, Holliday, Armitage, Kelly, Pounder, Cooper, Coverdale, Armstead. Front: Malpass, Harrison, Shaw, Rollin, F. Smith, Haigh, Chamberlain. Armour.

tackled, the loose forward hurled the ball back to Cooper. *'The wingman actually gathered the pass a split second before he had to jump over the prone figure of Chamberlain.'*

Cooper escaped the attentions of the Hunslet defence and scored near the posts to allow Frank Mortimer to add the extra two points and give Wakefield an unassailable 15-point lead.

With two minutes remaining Trinity took advantage of a tired Hunslet defence to score a super last try in a wonderful sweeping movement. Once again Holliday broke the defence and:

> *...gathering the ball, he twigged there was somebody rushing up behind him. It was full-back Mortimer who came sweeping through to take a well judged pass and so on to Bell, who drew the defence in astute fashion before handing on to Cooper to score the last points of the afternoon.*

It was a memorable victory in a fast, entertaining match that observers thought would go down in history as one of the best Yorkshire Challenge Cup finals ever staged.

Wakefield Trinity

F. Mortimer, Smith, A. Mortimer, Bell, Cooper, Holliday, Rollin, Harrison, Bridges, Haigh, Kelly, Armstead, Chamberlain

Tries: Smith 2, Cooper 2, A. Mortimer

Goals: F. Mortimer 4

Hunslet

Langton, Child, Stockdill, Waite, Preece, Gabitas, Talbot, Hatfield, Smith, Cooper, Shaw, Clues, Gunney

Try: Child

Goal: Talbot

Attendance: 31,000

Trinity join select company

Tour game at Belle Vue, 10 December 1956
Wakefield Trinity 17, Australia 12

The final club game of the disappointing Kangaroos tour brought their eighth defeat.

The game also marked the final appearance of the great Australian full-back Clive Churchill, who had played his last international game in the first Test at Wigan.

The encounter was marred by a series of injuries and, in the final minutes, two dismissals, but for all that it was never a particularly dirty game. The injuries to Australians Davies and Furner and Trinity's Bullock were the outcome of the accepted hazards of playing Rugby League football.

Front-row forward Davies received rib injuries in the 25th minute, while second-row forward Furner wrenched his shoulder within five minutes of the start of the second half. The *Yorkshire Post* commented:

> *Davies and Furner pluckily returned to the field after attention, but were useless trying to play with one arm each. After every allowance has been made for their ill luck they were a poor side and it would have a travesty of footballing justice if Trinity had lost.*

Wakefield and their 16-year-old debutant wing man Ken Hirst made a dream start to the match. The *Wakefield Express* described the try scored in the first two minutes:

> *Could any boy in his first game have pictured in his wildest dream that to him would go the distinction of scoring the first try of the afternoon and, more impor-*

Neil Fox, the complete footballer, who kicked four goals against the Australians.

tantly, in such rousing fashion. That sixty to seventy yards gallop from inside the Trinity half, including a moment when he nearly lost his pants when crashing through a tackle; and the kick and follow up for the touch down, thrilled every onlooker as much as it must have thrilled the ex-Morley Rugby Union winger.

The Australians won the majority of the first-half scrums but did little with the possession gained and failed to show any constructive ideas. Their defence was at times appalling and two basic errors led to tries for Trinity.

The usually ever-so-safe Australian full-back, Clive Churchill, dropped the ball almost on the line and Ken Rollin stepped in to gather and score in almost a single movement. Then Australia heeled cleanly from a scrum and when Connell failed to gather the ball Bullock nipped round to collect and score a grand opportunist try.

Shortly before half-time Connell scored a controversial try for the tourists:

> *From the press box it was difficult to follow the move on the far side of a scrum with a proper degree of certainty but Bullock appeared to have tackled Connell short of the line – a belief that was corroborated by Bullock during the interval.*

In the second half both team's defences were on top and there were no further tries scored. The Australians, perhaps due their injury problems, were shown great leniency in their methods by referee Mr Philpot. The *Wakefield Express* reporter was far from impressed by this and commented:

How did they get along without being penalised for some involuntary tackles and moves that bore more than a suspicion of obstruction tactics? And, apparently unnoticed, went a period when the Australians packed four forwards and had nine backs in action in contravention of the laws of the game which specify 'not more than eight players on each side shall act as backs'.

Two minutes before the end of the game, Australian forward Norm Provan was sent off for striking Armstead in a tackle. He was followed immediately afterwards by Shaw, for apparently applauding the referee's decision.

The following Saturday at Swinton, and without Davies and Provan, the Kangaroos were defeated 19–0 by Great Britain.

———————

Wakefield Trinity

Wilkins, F. Smith, Fox, Holliday, Hirst, Rollin, Bullock, Harrison, Shaw, Haigh, Kelly, Armstead, Chamberlain

Tries: Hirst, Rollin, Bullock

Goals: Fox 4

Australia

Churchill, Moir, Payne, O'Brien, Adams, Johnston, Connell, Furner, Hammerton, Davies, Purcell, Provan, Marsh

Tries: Johnson, Connell

Goals: Churchill 3

Attendance: 3,381

The toast is Trinity!

League match at Belle Vue, 1 February 1958
Wakefield Trinity 17, St Helens 12

In the mid-fifties the Wakefield club pledged itself to fast, open and attractive football and had placed its faith in a number of talented local players. The policy was a sound one, but the club also realised that they needed a number of first-class, skilful and, above all, experienced players to blend with the younger players. To do this they entered the transfer market and began a period of record-breaking activity.

In the 1957-58 season Wakefield signed, among others, the vastly experienced Coverdale, Metcalfe, Traill, Evans and Parker. They also signed Harold Poynton, a local player who had flirted with both Rugby League and soccer before spending two years in the Army.

A string of defeats in early 1958 worried the Trinity board; they needed a convincing victory to boost their plans for the future and the team's confidence.

The visit of League leaders St Helens to Belle Vue saw the club experiment with three new players. After just three appearances in the 'A' team, Poynton made his debut at stand-off, newly signed Reg Parker came in to the second row and reserve hooker Geoff Oakes was promoted to the first team for the first time.

St Helens were uncompromising opposition: they had trounced Trinity 52–5 at Knowsley Road in mid-December and were fully expected to do exactly the same at Belle Vue.

Neil Fox gave Wakefield a good start when he kicked a fine penalty goal in the second minute. The Trinity supporters' joy was short-lived though, and in the following 28 minutes St Helens tore Wakefield to pieces. Alex Murphy began the rout with a superb try, then Van Vollenhoven scored twice and Large swept in for a try in a frantic period. Wakefield were facing another pasting and were fortunate that not a single Saints try was converted.

With everything against them Trinity rallied, and, turning rout to revival, their forwards stood firm and began to battle back, meeting the St Helens six head-on in the middle of the

Trinity's side for the one of the finest performances of the season at Belle Vue. Back row: Chamberlain, Parker, Oakes, Lindley, Kelly, Harrison. Front row: Cooper, Smith, Rollin, Metcalfe, Lockwood, Poynton, Fox.

field. The *Wakefield Express* commented:

> *For physical endurance and a miraculous display of stamina in the almost uninterrupted clashes with the hefty visiting forwards, the work of the Wakefield six was something to be marvelled at.*

Four minutes from half-time, Trinity got the breakthrough their play deserved, when Rollin crossed for a try which Neil Fox converted. Wakefield's pack continued their strong work in the second half, and their display:

> *Galvanised the entire side into a fighting machine with a power to hit back in face of odds that would have knocked the heart out of many players.*

Trinity's entire style of play changed: scrums were won, passes were given at speed and players charged on to the ball, with every member of the team eager to work for the victory.

St Helens began to panic, with their play becoming increasingly erratic and untidy, in complete contrast to the stylish, rhythmic movements of their early work.

Four minutes into the second period Trinity drew level when Metcalfe crossed for a brilliant try which Fox converted.

Within 10 minutes Wakefield were in the lead, when 'a *polished exhibition of collaboration and amazing understanding between Poynton and Rollin*' created the gap for Neil Fox to score a try which he converted.

St Helens never recovered and Trinity were still searching for more points when the final whistle blew to end one of the finest games seen at Belle Vue for years. It would be a catalyst for a great revival in the club's fortunes.

Poynton's debut had been a revelation. One observer commented: '*he revealed pace, guile and all round natural footballing ability in quantities that marked him as a player who, most certainly, will go far.*' The other two debutantes, Oakes and Parker, had also played a big part in the victory, with the *Wakefield Express* reporting:

> *Could any onlooker, either Lancastrian or from the Yorkshire side of the Pennines, recollect a more conspicuously successful debut by three players on one side in the same match?*

Wakefield Trinity

Lockwood, Smith, Fox, Metcalfe, Cooper, Poynton, Rollin, Harrison, Oakes, Lindley, Kelly, Parker, Chamberlain

Tries: Metcalfe, Rollin, Fox

Goals: Fox 4

St Helens

Moses, Van Vollenhoven, Rhodes, Howard, Large, Price, Murphy, Prescott, McGuiness, Terry, Silcock, Robinson, Karalius

Tries: Murphy, Van Vollenhoven 2, Large

Attendance: 14,422

Clean, honest football

Challenge Cup first round at Knowsley Road, St Helens, 13 February 1960

St Helens 10, Wakefield Trinity 15

Trinity advanced into the second round of the cup with a superb all-round display in one of the most dramatic matches, brim full of twists and turns, for years.

The *Wakefield Express* wrote about the game:

> *Incredible! What better description could be applied to Wakefield's astonishing first round cup tie appearance at St Helens. From the kick-off they went about their task as if there wasn't a moment to spare. And in quick time the breathtaking pace they maintained completely changed the sort of afternoon out the local fan had contemplated.*

Trinity's attractive, open play was awesome and came as real shock to the Saints players and followers who had been expecting a typically dour cup-tie performance from Wakefield. Trinity varied their tactics to suit the obstacles impeding them, and thrilling individual thrusts gave way to precision passing movements completed at lightning speed.

Many Wakefield supporters had worried about John Etty's ability to contain the flying South African wing man Van Vollenhoven. Etty silenced his critics with a superb tactical display that muzzled the speedy winger's threat, and in addition he scored two superb tries. Fox and Etty combined to stop St Helens getting the ball to the wing and their spotting and tackling of Large and Vollenhoven was superb.

Neil Fox opened the scoring with a third-minute penalty, and then failed to convert John Etty's superb opening try. Fox landed a further penalty before St Helens hit back with a converted try from McGinn.

The cover from the match day programme.

The team line-ups from the match day programme.

Shortly before half-time Trinity were dealt a double blow when Round and Poynton collided with each other while going for a high ball. Both players were knocked unconscious and, faced with a precarious two-point lead and the possibility of being two men short, Trinity made a brave decision and carried on playing with their colleagues lying injured. Wakefield shocked the vast crowd with their tactics: no kick to touch, no deliberate technical offence to stop the game – they just continued to play and scored a sensational try.

It was a piece of daring to carry on playing as they did and it was a real turning point in the match. Round and Poynton received treatment while Fox was shaping up to attempt to convert Etty's second try. They both returned to the field with horrific injuries. Round had broken his jaw in two places and Poynton had a gash above his eye that needed four stitches. Neither player contemplated going off and continued to play.

Five minutes into the second half Wilkinson crossed for his first try for the club. Fox converted and Trinity had secured a five-point lead.

Wakefield's forwards were still playing a superb game:

Gerry Round, the Trinity full-back who had his jaw broken in the game.

Wilkinson, Vines, Turner and Oakes showed that St Helens had nothing better so far as loose play was concerned; Turner, in particular, was streets ahead of his international rival Karalius.

Eventually St Helens began to come back into the game and Rhodes scored a second which he converted himself. Trinity's defence held firm, however, with Poynton and Holliday playing superbly to contain both backs and forwards alike.

In the next rounds Trinity defeated Widnes and Whitehaven, and then Featherstone Rovers in the semi-final, to enter the final for the first time since that famous Wembley victory of 1946.

Wakefield Trinity

Round, F. Smith, Skene, Fox, Etty, Poynton, Holliday, Wilkinson, Oakes, Sampson, Vines, Firth, Turner

Tries: Wilkinson, Etty 2

Goals: Fox 3

St Helens

Rhodes, Van Vollenhoven, Large, McGinn, Prinsloo, W. Smith, Briers, A. Terry, Bowden, Prescott, Briggs, Huddart, Karalius

Tries: McGinn, Rhodes

Goals: Rhodes

Attendance: 29,000

Trinity the record breakers

Challenge Cup Final at Wembley, 14 May 1960
Hull 5, Wakefield Trinity 38

Trinity gave one of their finest displays of the season when, after a poor start, they tore Hull's defence to pieces in a second half that saw a series of bewildering moves to produce seven tries.

Harold Mather, writing in the *Guardian*, described the Wakefield performance:

> *Their display, though to Hull it must have appeared merciless, was delightful to watch. Passes were given and taken instantly and faultlessly; the backing up was an example for any textbook on the game; forwards dovetailed with backs (and vice versa) with an efficiency comparable with the splendid marching display given by the massed bands of the Guards; and yet when an individual thrust was called for always there was someone there to provide it.*

Derek Turner leads Trinity out for the club's first Wembley final since 1946.

The Hull side was far from representative of the Airlie Birds' successful season, as they were missing several key players through injury.

Wakefield took the initiative in the second minute with a penalty goal from Neil Fox, and within another two minutes Ken Rollin scored a superb solo try to put Trinity into a five-point lead.

Taking the advantage so early saw Wakefield adopt a strange policy, with the *Yorkshire Post* commenting:

> *Wakefield had the fidgets. They made things difficult for themselves by their reluctance to throw the ball about freely. This 'we must not lose' attitude is foreign to Trinity's style which thrives on adventurous passing and running.*

Hull began to gain in confidence and with Tom Harris's inspired running punching holes in the Trinity defence they began to play well. Harris's performance gave him the vote for the Lance Todd Trophy for the man of the match. The *Guardian* commented:

> *Rarely has one had the privilege of watching such a lion-hearted performance as the diminutive, likeable hooker gave, especially in the loose. The cause for which he was fighting was a lost one, but this made his efforts only the greater, and if had even one of his leg-weary colleagues managed to back him up in any time on*

South African centre Alan Skene looks round for support.

John Etty helps to stop Hull's John Whiteley.

Jack Wilkinson hauls down Mick Smith with a superb tackle.

any one of the four occasions when he made an outstandingly fine break Wakefield
at least would not have been able to call the tune as loudly as they did.

Hull's persistence came good, and from a scrum Cowan cleverly ran between his own half-backs and Broadhurst's surprise pass gave him the opening to score a well-worked try. Evans converted and Hull were level. Hull's injury problems continued when it was found that Cowan had broken a rib in the act of scoring and although he played on he took little part in the game.

Two minutes later another Neil Fox penalty goal restored Wakefield's lead. Ten minutes from half-time Harris received a bad injury and eventually left the field 15 minutes from the end of the game.

In the final 40 minutes Derek Turner, the Trinity captain, began to run amok and Wakefield ruthlessly exploited Hull's injury problems. Before Harris left the field Trinity swept in for four glorious long-range tries that tore the Hull defence to pieces. Holliday, Skene and Fox each scored a brace of tries in the second half: Keith Holliday's first was the hundredth try in Wembley finals. Three minutes from time Fred Smith scored a try which equalled the club's record of 37 in a season and Neil Fox created a Challenge Cup final record with a personal haul of 20 points when he converted Holliday's last try in the final minute of the game.

Derek Turner collected the Challenge Cup from Her Majesty Queen Elizabeth II, who was attending her first ever Challenge Cup Final.

Jack Wilkinson and Don Vines hoist Derek Turner shoulder high as a jubilant Trinity celebrate their record-breaking victory over Hull.

Wakefield Trinity

Round, Smith, Skene, Fox, Etty, Rollin, Holliday, Wilkinson, Oakes, Vines, Firth, Chamberlain, Turner

Tries: Rollin, Fox 2, Skene 2, Holliday 2, Smith

Goals: Fox 7

Hull

Kershaw, Harrison, Cowan, Halafhi, Johnson, Broadhurst, Finn, Scott, Harris, Evans, Sutton, Smith, Whiteley

Try: Cowan

Goal: Evans

Attendance: 79,773

GREAT GAMES: 28

Entertaining football

Yorkshire Challenge Cup Final at Headingley, 29 October 1960
Huddersfield 10, Wakefield Trinity 16

Wakefield had defeated Halifax in a dour 3–0 game at Belle Vue in the first round of the Cup. They then trounced Bramley 40–6 before beating Keighley by a single point in the semi-final. Huddersfield had beaten Batley 20–2 at Mount Pleasant, then Castleford 15–3 before grinding out a tough win against favourites Leeds at Headingley.

Trinity never looked like losing their 14th Yorkshire Cup Final even when Huddersfield seemed to gain the initiative when they drew level.

Huddersfield's forwards played a magnificent game in defence and it was thought by many that the Trinity pack was a poor second to the Fartown six. The *Wakefield Express* was quite scathing about the Trinity forwards, writing:

> *Again Trinity followers were treated to the sight of forwards getting plenty of the ball from the scrums but who did little else towards assisting their backs to penetrate the opposition's defence.*

The Huddersfield defence took some cracking, however, although:

> *Rollin, Poynton and Fox, with some occasional smart work from Metcalfe from the full-back position, were the men who showed the brightest prospects of finding a way through the ranks of the Huddersfield defence.*

After eight minutes play a clever back-flip from Poynton put Skene over the line, only to be recalled for an offence, then Rollin burst through and found Turner with a lovely long pass. The Trinity captain came close but the Huddersfield cover got across to him to snuff out the danger.

Wakefield broke the deadlock in the 10th minute when Fred Smith's fingertips intercepted an Ashcroft pass bound for Breen. The wing man juggled with the ball, gained control and sprinted 30 yards for a fine opportunist try. Neil Fox converted the try.

Trinity captain Derek Turner
collects the Yorkshire
Challenge Cup.

Seven minutes later Breen crossed for Huddersfield and then five minutes before the interval Fox hoisted a huge kick towards the Fartowners' line. Full-back Dyson was beaten by a cruel bounce of the ball and Fox gathered his own kick to score a try which he converted.

Huddersfield hit back with a penalty goal from Dyson and then Breen stepped neatly past two Trinity defenders and passed to Lockwood, who crossed for a try to which Dyson added the two points.

Huddersfield were level but seemed to be content to hold on for a draw, and allowed Wakefield to take the initiative. Trinity's third try came from a well-timed long pass from Briggs to Etty, who '... *used his strength and great determination in forcing a passage near the corner.*' Briggs was one of the few forwards singled out for praise:

> *In that below par Wakefield pack, Briggs was about the only one to be sufficiently effective in a constructive sense to attract attention.*

With two minutes to go before full-time, Neil Fox crowned a clever and skilful personal performance when he intercepted a pass on the Huddersfield 25-yard line and dashed over the line to ground the ball directly under the crossbar. It was *'A position from which he astonished onlookers by failing to kick the goal'*.

It was the final score of the match. Wakefield had won the Yorkshire Challenge Cup for the first time since 1956.

———————

Wakefield Trinity
Metcalfe, F. Smith, Skene, Fox, Etty, Poynton, Rollin, Wilkinson, Oakes, Chamberlain, Briggs, Firth, Turner
Tries: Smith, Fox 2, Etty
Goals: Fox 2

Huddersfield
Dyson, Brown, Curry, Ashcroft, Breen, Lockwood, Smales, Slevin, Close, Noble, Devereux, Bowman, Valentine
Tries: Breen, Lockwood
Goals: Dyson 2

Attendance: 17,456

101

Fox's kicking crucial

Challenge Cup Final at Wembley, 12 May 1962
Huddersfield 6 Wakefield Trinity 12

Wakefield, despite having already collected the Yorkshire Cup and League trophies, were far from favourites to defeat Huddersfield. The *Guardian* commented:

> *Although Wakefield appear to carry all the big guns individually Huddersfield's collective ammunition will take a great deal of subduing.*

The Fartowners' unflagging determination and enthusiasm was considered, by the majority of newspaper pundits, to be enough to defeat a Trinity side lacking Vines and Kosanovic.

Wakefield and Huddersfield stride across the Wembley pitch for the pre-match ceremonies.

THE RUGBY LEAGUE CHALLENGE CUP COMPETITION

FINAL TIE

HUDDERSFIELD

v

WAKEFIELD TRINITY

SATURDAY, MAY 12th, 1962   KICK-OFF 3 p.m.

EMPIRE STADIUM

WEMBLEY

OFFICIAL PROGRAMME   -   ONE SHILLING

Trinity hooker Geoff Oakes is tackled by three Huddersfield players.

Both sides scored two tries, but the telling balance of power in Trinity's favour came from Neil Fox, who dropped three goals, scored a try and constantly troubled the Huddersfield defence. Fox's outstanding achievement won him the Lance Todd Trophy for man of the match:

> *... not only was he, considering the place and the occasion, remarkably calm when making his drops at goal but had the thrust and a strong hand off which helped considerably when making the first inroads into Huddersfield's tight knit defence.*

Wakefield's grip on the game was deep rooted; they showed far more method, their play was quicker, and as one observer put it: *'the game only seemed to come alive when Wakefield were on the move.'*

Second row forward Brian Briggs had a great game. His tackling at close range and towards the flanks was superb, and on the attack he was outstanding:

> *... so finely did Briggs spot the half openings and so well, having often darted through them, did he then link with his backs that he was outstanding.*

Ken Hirst, Trinity's flying wing man, is stopped in his tracks by Huddersfield full back Dyson.

However, Wakefield's victory was built on solid team work and sound backing up by all 13 players. Huddersfield were beaten almost everywhere for speed, but their tactics did little to help their play. Far too often, instead of opening out play, the ball was turned back inside, usually to a forward.

Trinity opened the scoring in the 17th minute when Fox dropped his first goal. Just before the kick Turner was badly injured and left the field for 10 minutes to be treated for concussion. In the 20th minute Fox ran straight through his opposing centre, Booth, passed to Hirst, then

Wakefield full-back Gerry Round is tackled.

followed up on the outside to take the return pass and score in the corner. He failed with the conversion.

Huddersfield, aided with more possession from scrums, kept plugging away and were rewarded in the 30th minute when quick passing sent the ball to the wing, where Smales beat Round on the outside to score. Dyson missed with the goal attempt.

On the hour, Turner transferred the ball to Fox, who once again steadied himself to kick a wonderful drop-goal. A minute later Briggs slipped a subtle pass to Hirst, who raced from his own 25-yard line past two defenders, side-stepped Dyson and beat the pursuing Smales to score a fine try.

Huddersfield loose forward Ramsden gave the Fartowners a glimmer of hope with a try three minutes from time, but with seconds to go before the final whistle, Turner once again passed to Fox, who calmly dropped his third goal.

It was the final act of the game. Trinity had won the Challenge Cup for the fourth time in their history.

The game was an unusual one in that it was the first Wembley Final to be decided without a single successful place kick, and Neil Fox became the first player in a final to land three drop-goals.

The following week Huddersfield's Frank Dyson, who had failed five place kicks, was successful with four against Trinity in the Championship Final at Odsal Stadium.

Turner and the cup are hoisted again as Trinity celebrate at Wembley for the second time in two years.

Wakefield Trinity

Round, Smith, Skene, Fox, Hirst, Poynton, Holliday, Wilkinson, Oakes, Firth, Briggs, Williamson, Turner

Tries: Fox, Hirst

Goals: Fox 3

Huddersfield

Dyson, Breen, Booth, Haywood, Wicks, Deighton, Smales, Slevin, Close, Noble, Clarke, Bowman, Ramsden

Tries: Smales, Ramsden

Attendance: 81,263

Trinity 'foxed' Wigan

League match at Belle Vue, 24 February 1962
Wakefield Trinity 14, Wigan 11

A huge crowd of 27,614, a post-war record for Belle Vue, witnessed the first 'Battle of the Giants' between the first and second clubs in the League. The gates were locked and the atmosphere at Belle Vue resembled a Cup Final when the teams, including 16 internationals, took the field.

Wigan, seeking their 18th victory in succession, were at full strength, with Cherrington preferred to Lyon in the second row. Trinity, undefeated in their last 24 games, were without Vines, Greenwood, Prinsloo and Kosanovic.

Wakefield took the lead in the fifth minute, when Neil Fox kicked a penalty goal from three yards inside the Wigan half. In the 13th minute Wigan were swept aside when, from a scrum, Wakefield came away in classical fashion:

> *Poynton served Fox and Trinity's Test centre delayed his pass astutely as Davies tacked. Round, backing up, took the pass and sailed up the wing with Hirst coming inside for the return pass which he took to gallop over. Fox converted to give Wakefield a 7-nil lead.*

It was the start that Trinity and their thousands of followers had hoped for. The initial worry about the strength of the Wigan pack was fading, and in the scrums Geoff Oakes was doing a great job, heeling cleanly on a regular basis.

The boot of Fox put Wakefield further ahead with a penalty when McTigue was found guilty of robbing Firth. Wigan gained ground with a long-range touch-finding penalty from Griffiths and then moved to within 10 yards of the line with another superb kick. Davies raced through towards the line, and Round halted him, but a penalty at the play the ball gave Griffiths the chance to make it 9–2.

Trinity's five players for the 1962 tour of Australia and New Zealand, who all played a big part in the defeat of Wigan. Left to right: Gerry Round, Jack Wilkinson, Neil Fox, Derek Turner and Harold Poynton.

Wigan continued to press the Trinity line and Round was forced to kick the ball dead. From the drop out:

> *Fox gathered his own kick and stormed away. He went past half way and sent Griffiths the wrong way, only to find the referee had blown to where the run had started.*

It was a blow to Wakefield because the certain 'five-pointer' would have given Trinity a 14–2 lead. The protests from the crowd were silenced when, from the scrum:

> *Wigan moved the ball swiftly across to Carlton. He took his chance as Trinity's defence hesitated and went over, with Wilkinson hanging on, for a try.*

Griffiths converted superbly to put Wigan within two points. At the start of the second half Griffiths brought the scores level with a penalty kick. Wigan now had a monopoly of possession from the scrums, with the *Wakefield Express* commenting:

> *… that, most likely would have not occurred if Geoff Oakes had not sustained a severe buffeting in a heavy double tackle.*

Wigan were now attacking well. Ashton and Davies came close and Bolton probed the Trinity defence. With around 10 minutes left to play Griffiths gave Wigan the lead with his fourth penalty of the afternoon.

Wakefield were tiring, Wilkinson was limping and twice Oakes received attention. But then, with five minutes left to play, Oakes hooked the ball from a scrum:

> *... the ball sped via Poynton, Fox and Skene to Smith on the wing. He straightened down the touch and sped towards Wigan's line. Fox, sensing the victory chance, went with him for the return pass. It came twenty yards out and the centre took it to move in for a try without a defender getting near him.*

Fox converted to give Trinity a 14–11 lead. The final whistle blew with Hirst held just short of the line.

The victory gave Wakefield a League record of 20 victories, one draw and a solitary defeat and put them one point behind leaders Wigan with a game in hand.

Trinity ended the season joint top of the League with Wigan. They defeated Featherstone Rovers 13–8 in the play-off semi-finals, then lost 5–14 to Huddersfield in the Championship Final at Odsal Stadium, Bradford. A victory that May afternoon would have given Wakefield

The Rugby Leaguer makes the Wakefield v Wigan game front page news.

their fourth trophy of the season and equalled the feats of Hunslet, Huddersfield and Swinton in winning 'all four Cups'.

Wakefield Trinity

Round, Smith, Skene, Fox, Hirst, Poynton, Holliday, Wilkinson, Oakes, Williamson, Firth, Briggs, Turner

Tries: Hirst, Fox

Goals: Fox 4

Wigan

Griffiths, Boston, Ashton, Davies, Carlton, Bolton, Parr, Barton, Sayer, McTigue, Collier, Cherrington, Evans

Try: Carlton

Goals: Griffiths 4

Attendance: 27,614

Wakefield Trinity win worthily

Challenge Cup Final at Wembley, 11 May 1963
Wakefield Trinity 25, Wigan 10

Wigan had been installed as firm favourites to win the Challenge Cup well before the teams met at Wembley. Many experts admitted that Trinity would have an advantage at half-back with Holliday and Poynton, but Wigan's teamwork was thought to be the deciding factor.

Wigan began their eighth Wembley Final oozing with the confidence of favourites, and launched themselves into the game with a series of fierce assaults on the Trinity line.

Wakefield defended superbly, their forwards met Wigan's pack head on in the centre of the field and the pace of the backs had everything covered out wide. As the game progressed Wigan faltered, and Trinity began to launch their own attacks with a speed and precision that Wigan were unable to match.

At the heart of these movements were half-backs Harold Poynton and Keith Holliday, whose skill, craft and speed were simply too much for Wigan to handle. Poynton, who won the Lance Todd trophy, was the 'white pimpernel' – Wigan sought him here, there and everywhere, and found him nowhere. The *Daily Herald* wrote of his display: '*It is rare that you get such a lavish display of skill and showmanship as Poynton turned in*'.

Minutes before the break Wigan were dealt two major blows, their defence finally cracking when Sampson romped over for a try under the sticks, which Neil Fox converted. Within a minute their influential full-back Dave Bolton was badly concussed and was receiving attention when the teams left the field for half-time.

Wigan returned without Bolton but opened their scoring in the first minute of the second half when Pitchford scored an unconverted try. Trinity soon recovered and Gert 'Oupa' Coetzer flashed down the wing to score in the corner. Fox added the two points with a superb touchline

Malcolm Sampson opens the scoring with a superb try.

Man of the match Harold Poynton is stopped by a Wigan defender. Ian Brooke (left) and Don Vines are in support.

A smiling Jack Wilkinson collects his medal from Field-Marshal Montgomery.

conversion. Bolton returned to the fray but Wigan were by now a demoralised team; Trinity's awesome pace and flair in attack was beginning to tell:

> *Gone were the understanding and zest of their forwards in the loose. The gaps often found in the Wigan defence were remarkable.*

Ashton landed a penalty to pull Wigan within five points and then a minute later Neil Fox kicked a penalty to stretch the Trinity lead again. Ashton again reduced the lead with another fine penalty in the 65th minute.

In the 68th minute Bolton made a fine break and then launched a pass back inside for Ashton. Poynton covered the break and, instead of moving in to tackle Ashton, held back for a split second to intercept the pass and scamper over the line for a glorious try.

Wigan found the energy to briefly hit back and Collier forced his way over for a try in the corner. The score meant little: Wakefield were in complete control and with two minutes remaining Coetzer scored his second try in the corner. Fox missed the conversion.

In the final seconds of the game 20-year-old centre Ian Brooke scored Wakefield's final try, which Neil Fox converted.

Wakefield's convincing victory astounded the critics. The *Guardian* commented:

> It was, perhaps, the standard of Wakefield's teamwork which was the surprising factor of all, for such an asset was considered to be Wigan's prerogative. Holliday and Poynton showed skills beyond that anticipated and the rest of their colleagues rose magnificently to their task. The absence, through concussion, of Bolton for the first 17 minutes of the second half certainly handicapped the losers; nevertheless it must not be allowed to detract from the merit of Wakefield's performance. Indeed, this was all the more remarkable in that they heeled from only one of what few scrums there were in the second half – yet scored four tries during the period.

Trinity's players and officials were given a rapturous welcome when they returned to Wakefield with the Cup for the third time in four years, with thousands lining the streets.

....

Wakefield Trinity

Round, Greenwood, Brooke, Fox, Coetzer, Poynton, Holliday, Wilkinson, Kosanovic, Sampson, Vines, Turner, Pearman

Tries: Sampson, Coetzer 2, Poynton, Brooke

Goals: Fox 5

Wigan

Bolton, Boston, Ashton, Davies, Carlton, McLeod, Pitchford, Barton, Sayer, McTigue, Collier, Lyon, Evans

Tries: Pitchford, Collier

Goals: Ashton 2

Attendance: 84,492

Jack Wilkinson and Derek Turner parade the trophy. Both forwards played in all three of Trinity's Wembley successes in the early 1960s.

Trinity celebrate their famous victory over Wigan, their third Wembley win in four years.

This great Trinity team

Tour match at Belle Vue, 30 October 1965
Wakefield Trinity 16, New Zealand 4

The Kiwis played their final club fixture of the 23-match tour against Wakefield at Belle Vue. The New Zealanders performed much better than the Kiwis of 1961, who lost 12 of their 20 games. Before coming to Wakefield the New Zealanders had been defeated in four of their fixtures against clubs, and had beaten Lancashire.

The two tries Trinity scored hardly gave a fair reflection of the game, in which they never looked like being beaten.

The New Zealand captain, Billy Snowden, congratulated Wakefield on being by far the best footballing side the tourists had encountered on the tour. The *Wakefield Express* commented on the afternoon:

> *In a gale force wind and some heavy rain, it was not always an exciting afternoon's affair. But there was plenty to please even though there was disappointment at the lack of ability shown by the almost Test strength Kiwis combination.*

Neil Fox had a superb game, the centre kicking five goals and scoring a try, and was thought by many of the onlookers to be the man of the match. The award, sponsored by a major tobacco company, went to his centre partner Willis Rushton. The *Wakefield Express* reported:

> *It was earned by his eighty minutes non-stop endeavour. The ball went the way of Rushton quite a lot and although there were occasions when mishandling spoiled the show, his ceaseless probing found ways through the defence that put him in the top class as an attacker. With an extra yard in a 100 Willis would on two occasions have gone on through openings of his own making to score.*

The programme for the game against New Zealand at Belle Vue.

Trinity's forwards excelled throughout the game and when Derek Turner had to leave the field with concussion in the 16th minute, the pack continued to take the game to the tourists. Turner's place was taken by substitute Noel Dalton, who quickly showed impressive form.

Wakefield's prop forwards had good, solid games:

How about the Wakefield props being in the running for tour trials? Both Edgar Bate and Ted Campbell rendered yeoman service. They got on with a prop's work in the rucks instead of seeking the limelight and making a hash of duties assigned to the backs. From many skirmishes well timed passes were sent out by the Wakefield men.

For Trinity Neil Fox and Ken Batty scored tries and Neil Fox kicked five goals. For the New Zealanders Fagin and Tait landed penalty goals.

The following Saturday the New Zealanders drew 9–9 with Great Britain in the third and final test match at Central Park, Wigan.

Wakefield Trinity

Metcalfe, Thomas, Rushton, N. Fox, Garthwaite, Batty, Holliday, Bate, Shepherd, Campbell, Turner (Dalton), Haigh, D. Fox

Tries: Batty, N. Fox

Goals: N. Fox 5

New Zealand

Fagan, Reidy, Kennedy, Tait, Langton, Bailey, Snowdon, Edwards, Shultz, Emery, Orchard, Dixon, Deacon

Goals: Fagan, Tait

Attendance: 7,484

Derek Turner, Trinity's international forward, who had to leave the field.

Wakefield Trinity worthy Rugby League champions

Championship Final replay at Station Road, Swinton, 10 May 1967

St Helens 9, Wakefield Trinity 21

Wakefield had striven for over 70 years to be crowned Rugby League Champions. In 1960 Trinity ended the season in second place with 32 victories in 38 games. They trounced Hull 24–4 in the play-off semi-final and then were beaten 3–27 by Wigan at Odsal Stadium. Two seasons later Wakefield were joint League leaders with Wigan, and defeated Featherstone Rovers 13–8 in the semi-final. In the final, again at Odsal Stadium, Trinity lost to Huddersfield, the team they had beaten in the Challenge Cup Final the week before. The final against Huddersfield was the last in the top four play-off system to decide who would be the League Champions.

In 1967 Trinity ended the season in third position and then defeated Salford, Workington and Hull Kingston Rovers in the semi-final at Craven Park.

Trinity went in to the Final as narrow favourites; they had lost one game since Christmas, and had overpowered a very capable Hull Kingston Rovers side in the semi-final. Trinity were determined to win the Championship for the first time.

Torrential rain and hail pounded Headingley just before the kick-off, leaving large pools of water all over the pitch. Early tackles brought huge sprays of water as the players slipped around the sodden turf. St Helens mastered the conditions well in the first half and a try from prop Watson and two Killeen goals gave the Saints a 7–2 lead.

Trinity fought back: Fox kicked a penalty and a controversial obstruction try was awarded when Bolton pulled Ray Owen back as he tried to reach a kick-through. Amid another bout of thunder and heavy rain, Neil Fox hit the upright with his conversion attempt. The scores remained at 7–7, forcing a replay at Swinton.

Trinity's 1967 Championship squad. Back row: Coetzer, Bath, Neil Fox, Clarkson, Campbell, Haigh, Shepherd, D. Fox, Batty. Front row: Prior, Owen, Poynton, Cooper, Brooke, Hirst.

Both sides were unchanged for the replay, although there was a new referee. Mr G. Philpott withdrew from the match when his wife received a series of anonymous threatening letters; Mr J. Manley of Warrington took over.

Conditions at Swinton were in direct contrast to those at Leeds. It was a glorious sunny evening and the firm pitch gave Trinity the ideal conditions for their speedy backs.

From the kick-off, hooker Bernard Prior began to heel from the scrums at a two to one rate, giving Poynton and Owen, who won the man of the match award, the possession they missed at Headingley. Don Fox's superb strategic kicking gave Wakefield a tremendous advantage and within 20 minutes Trinity were in a 6–2 lead following tries from Owen and Brooke.

Saints pulled into the lead with a Bishop drop-goal and a try from Van Vollenhoven, but following a quick play the ball from Owen, Poynton darted over for a try which Neil Fox converted.

Early in the second half Killeen landed a penalty to narrow the gap, but the two points merely spurred Trinity on to another wave of high-speed movements. Owen, Poynton and Bob Haigh combined to give Brooke the chance to dummy his way past two men and race over for his second try, which Neil Fox converted. By now Wakefield were in almost complete control, and the *Daily Express* commented:

Trinity dominated this all action replayed final almost from beginning to end. They did it by superb, slick, open football which contrasted vividly with Saints' more forward conscience stuff.

The Trophy was won when Poynton mounted a superb run down the right wing. He drew three men away from Hirst, then passed to the wing man for him to score Wakefield's final try. Neil Fox missed the conversion but later kicked a penalty goal to give Trinity a 21–9 victory and the coveted Championship Trophy for the first time in their long and proud history.

The players who won the Championship at Headingley never once played together again, as a mixture of injuries and transfers prevented all 13 from taking the field together as a team.

Wakefield Trinity

Cooper, Hirst, Brooke, N. Fox, Coetzer, Poynton, Owen, Bath, Prior, Campbell, Clarkson, Haigh, D. Fox

Tries: Brooke 2, Hirst, Owen, Poynton

Goals: N. Fox 3

St Helens

F. Barrow, Van Vollenhoven, A. Barrow, Smith, Killeen, Douglas, Bishop, Warlow, Sayer, Watson, French, Hogan, Mantle

Try: Van Vollenhoven

Goals: Bishop, Killeen 2

Attendance: 33,537

Aye, it's Trinity for Cup second round

Challenge Cup First Round at Craven Park, Barrow,
3 February 1968

Barrow 4, Wakefield Trinity 8

A magnificent defensive display gave League champions Wakefield the victory in a tough, hard-fought game on the Cumbrian coast.

Trinity were never behind in the game but Barrow were a tough, uncompromising side to overcome, as the *Wakefield Express* commented:

> *… it will be seen that Wakefield were never able to tear themselves out of the relentless grip of Barrow, not enough to allow the big crowd of Belle Vue followers to breathe contentedly. Always there was the possibility of a try being scored by the home side in the right spot for a goal to be added.*

The game was an exceedingly tough, characteristic cup tie, with several of the experienced Wakefield players guilty of giving away penalty kicks to Barrow in moments of crisis when coolness under pressure was expected. As early as the fifth minute old hand Don Fox decided to argue with York-based referee Hebblethwaite when he was caught in an offside position by the touch judge. Tees, the Barrow full-back, missed the kick.

Trinity took the lead in the 23rd minute when, *'with a fine piece of opportunism,'* Cumbrian-born Joe Bonner scored a fine try. Neil Fox added the two points with a fine conversion. But things did not all go according to plan, as one observer described:

> *Even skipper Harold Poynton afforded Barrow two points when he toppled second*

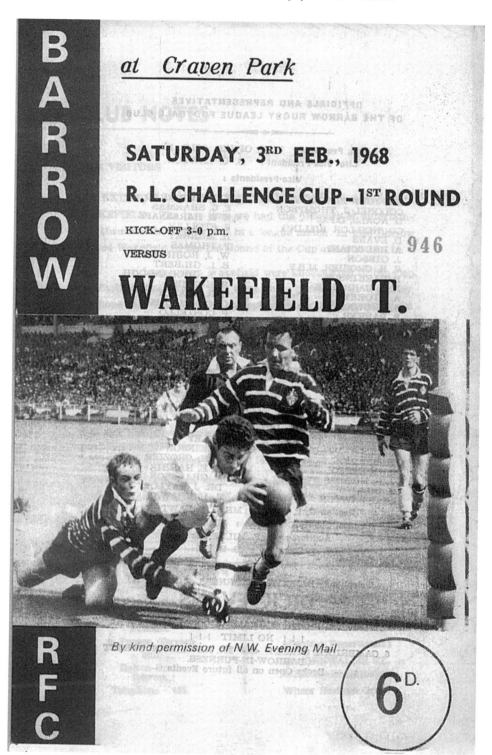

The cover from the official match day programme.

row forward Tomlinson with a head high tackle that brought gasps from
spectators.

Barrow full-back Tees kicked the penalty and the Cumbrians were just three points adrift. In the second half, hooker Geoff Oakes continued to hold his own in the scrums but was the victim of several strange decisions. The *Wakefield Express* commented:

> *Geoff Oakes finished up only 14-15 in gaining possession on the full game, but it*
> *was difficult from long distance viewing to know why when the ball came out on*
> *the Wakefield's side of scrums that referee Hebblethwaite was dissatisfied and*
> *ordered another scrum. For this reason Oakes was deprived of being well in the*
> *lead in gaining possession.*

Trinity continued to question the Barrow defence, but the Cumbrian side were also adept at mounting their own attacks and from one of these forays Halliwell dropped a goal to pull the lead back to a single point.

Gradually Barrow began to exert a vice-like grip on the game and in the final 20 minutes:

> *… they pitched in with everything they possessed to bolster up frenzied waves of*
> *assaults that had the Wakefield supporters biting their nails and counting the*
> *seconds left to play.*

On the hour Don Fox sold a brilliant dummy to crash over the line for a try. The extra two points on offer were missed but Trinity had a slender lead which they determined to hold on to. In the final stages of the game Wakefield's defence 'bordered on the miraculous' in the face of an increasingly tough and frustrated Barrow side:

> *… when one defender faulted, praise be, there was another there to fill the gap*
> *before the attackers could drive home their initial advantage. Phew! That was the*
> *real Trinity that was.*

The result was in doubt until the last seconds, when Trinity held on and were worthy winners of one of their hardest cup ties for many a season.

In the second round they defeated Salford at The Willows and then beat Castleford 18–5 at

Matt McLeod, the Cumbrian forward who had a great game at Barrow.

Belle Vue to set up a semi-final with Huddersfield. The first semi-final was a dour scoreless draw, but Huddersfield were overcome 15–10 in the Headingley replay to set up a Challenge Cup Final appearance against Leeds.

In one of the strangest and most controversial finals in the history of the Challenge Cup competition, Trinity were defeated by a single point in a game that was played in the most atrocious weather conditions imaginable.

Wakefield Trinity

Cooper, Coetzer, Brooke, N. Fox, Batty, Poynton, Bonnar, Jeanes, Oakes, D. Fox, Haigh, McLeod, Hawley

Tries: Bonner, D. Fox

Goal: N. Fox

Barrow

Tees, Wear, Douglas, Shuttleworth, Murray, Brophy, Smith, Halliwell, Wright, Hopwood, Sanderson, Tomlinson, Kirchin

Goals: Tees, Halliwell

Attendance: 10,437

Wakefield forwards in control

Championship Final at Headingley, Leeds, 4 May 1968
Hull Kingston Rovers 10, Wakefield Trinity 17

Trinity looked anything but Champions at the start of the 1967-68 campaign. Incredible bad luck with injuries decimated the side and they were successful in only seven of their first 16 games. The Trinity officials looked to the transfer market to strengthen the side and signed David Jeanes, Matt McLeod and Joe Bonner and moved Don Fox to prop forward. The new signings blended in well and following a brilliant run of victories, Wakefield finished the season in second place in the League table with 24 wins and a draw in their 34 games. In the play-offs they defeated Huddersfield and Castleford to set up a semi-final against Wigan at Belle Vue. Trinity triumphed 26–9 over Wigan, for whom Billy Boston played his last game, to enter their second successive Championship Final.

Hull Kingston Rovers were installed as favourites to take Trinity's title but despite winning more than adequate possession, Rovers were taken apart by a Wakefield side at the top of its form. Harold Mather, writing in the *Guardian*, commented:

> *It has been said of this Wakefield side that they are a machine. And in this form they are. Mastering such fundamentals as covering and tackling and the giving and taking of passes, they rarely make a mistake.*

Trinity opened the scoring when sheer speed and backing-up put Owen in for a try which Neil Fox converted. Millward kicked a penalty goal and then, following a long period of defence, Rovers cut loose from the Wakefield cover and Longstaff scored in the corner.

Foster had been a danger to Trinity with some clever, well-timed passes to set up teammates

The cover from the official match day programme.

HULL KINGSTON ROVERS
Colours: Red jerseys with white collar, white shorts

1.	DAVID WAINWRIGHT	Full Back
2.	CHRIS YOUNG*	Right Wing
3.	JOHN MOORE	Right Centre
4.	ALAN BURWELL*	Left Centre
5.	PAUL LONGSTAFF	Left Wing
6.	ROGER MILLWARD*	Out Half
7.	COLIN COOPER	Scrum Half
8.	LES FOSTER	Front Row Forward
9.	PETER FLANAGAN*	Hooker
10.	BRIAN MENNELL	Front Row Forward
11.	PHIL LOWE	Second Row Forward
12.	TERRY MAJOR	Second Row Forward
13.	FRANK FOSTER* (Capt.)	Loose Forward
14.	PHIL COUPLAND	Substitute
15.	BILL HOLLIDAY*	Substitute

THE TEAMS

40 minutes' play in each half
10-minute interval

In the event of a draw after 80 minutes, the replay will be at Headingley, Leeds, on Wednesday, 8th May, 1968, kick-off 7.30 p.m. Seating tickets at £1 and 15/- and North Stand Enclosure tickets at 6/6d. can be obtained from either of the competing clubs or from the Leeds C.F. & A.C. Ltd.

Music before the game and at half-time will be played by the City of Leeds Police Band (by kind permission of the Chief Constable, James Angus, Esq.)

WAKEFIELD TRINITY
Colours: White jerseys with narrow red and blue "V", white shorts

1.	GARY COOPER	Full Back
2.	DAVID GARTHWAITE	Right Wing
3.	IAN BROOKE* NEIL FOX*	Right Centre
4.	GERT COETZER	Left Centre
5.	KEN BATTY	Left Wing
6.	HAROLD POYNTON* (Capt.)	Out Half
7.	RAY OWEN	Scrum Half
8.	DAVID JEANES	Front Row Forward
9.	GEORGE SHEPHERD	Hooker
10.	DON FOX*	Front Row Forward
11.	MATT McLEOD	Second Row Forward
12.	BOB HAIGH	Second Row Forward
13.	DAVID HAWLEY	Loose Forward
14.	GEOFF. CLARKSON	Substitute
15.	TED CAMPBELL	Substitute

* denotes Great Britain International

Referee: D. S. BROWN (Preston)   Touch Judges: H. WALTON (Dewsbury), J. W. JOWETT (Leeds)

The team line-ups from the official match day programme.

supporting his breaks. Trinity sensed the danger quickly and marked the threatening player much more closely. Almost immediately the spark of inspiration seemed to leave the Hull Kingston Rovers players.

The sides turned round all square, but with the wind behind them Trinity were soon in the lead. Ex-Wakefield Rugby Union prop David Jeanes barged through three defenders to crash over for a try, to which Neil Fox added the two points.

Rovers continued to press the Trinity line, but:

> ... *faced by a side that covered and tackled so quickly and soundly that they were never allowed to get into their stride or rhythm, they were made to look very ordinary. Certainly they seemed bereft of ideas of how to get round Wakefield's close marking.*

Millward dropped a goal for Rovers but by now Owen and Poynton were combining to create havoc in the Hull defence. Coupled with this two-pronged threat were:

> ... *the speed, the skill, and the sense of judgement of Gary Cooper's joining of*

movements which often punched the holes that mattered. Hull Kingston must have wondered where he would 'bob' up next.

The Wakefield full-back's superb display in both defence and on the attack earned him the Harry Sunderland Trophy as man of the match.

Neil Fox scored a try which his brother Don converted, and then Poynton calmly dropped a goal.

Hull Kingston Rovers centre Moore scored a late try, which Millward converted, but the trophy was on its way back to Wakefield. The *Daily Express* summed up the game with these comments:

> *Once again yet another wonderful Wakefield performance has confounded the forecast. But there are no moans from me for Trinity's tremendous league title retaining effort made them most worthy additions to the list of six clubs who have previously won the title in two successive seasons.*

———

Wakefield Trinity

Cooper, Coetzer, Brooke, N. Fox, Batty, Poynton, Owen, Jeanes, Shepherd, D. Fox, Haigh, McLeod, Hawley

Tries: Owen 2, N. Fox, Jeanes

Goals: N. Fox 2, Poynton, D. Fox

Hull Kingston Rovers

Wainwright, Young, Moore, Burwell, Longstaff, Millward, Cooper, Foster, Flanagan, Mennell, Lowe, Major, Foster

Tries: Moore, Longstaff

Goals: Millward 2

Attendance: 22,586

A shining star in Belle Vue's gloom

League match at Belle Vue, Wakefield, 7 January 1972
Wakefield Trinity 22, Huddersfield 4

Belle Vue on a cold, damp and murky Sunday afternoon in midwinter could hardly be called hospitable. However, not all great games and great performances are played on beautiful, warm days and not all are played in the perfect surroundings of Wembley Stadium.

The brave souls who left the comforts of a warm fireside were treated to a fine game of Rugby League football and a stunning display from David Topliss.

Topliss had, by his own high standards, had a very quiet start to the season, often playing out of position, but against Huddersfield he excelled. The *Wakefield Express* commented on the stand-off:

> *Topliss has hit top form and must surely be attracting the international selectors' attention. His speed and eye for an opening made his display outstanding on a day when most players were struggling to cope with the greasy conditions.*

Trinity were in 10th place in the League table, having won 11 of their 18 games. Huddersfield, who had not scored a try in three games, were four points below Wakefield in the table.

Trinity took the lead after three minutes of play when Neil Fox kicked a penalty, awarded when Huddersfield were caught offside. Six minutes later Davies missed a chance to equalise when he hooked his penalty attempt wide of the posts.

Trinity scored their first try when a superb, well judged, long pass from Neil Fox split open the Huddersfield defence. Topliss took the ball well and scampered over for a try which Fox converted.

Huddersfield pressed the Trinity line and were awarded a penalty when Wakefield were caught offside directly in front of their own posts. Davies landed the penalty and minutes later Huddersfield full-back Wallace dropped a superb goal to pull back Trinity's lead to three points.

Huddersfield continued to worry the Wakefield defence and shortly before half-time they were attacking well. From well inside his own half, Topliss managed to slip through an opening and made a fine break. Hegarty supported the break and sped down the field before returning the ball to Topliss, who sped over the line for his 50th try for Wakefield. Neil Fox converted and at half-time Trinity had a somewhat flattering 12–4 lead.

Four minutes into the second half Wakefield made the game safe when they began to take the game to Huddersfield:

> *... there seemed to be no danger when Valentine was held by two defenders 30 yards out, but he managed to slip the ball to Topliss who romped over again.*

Fox kicked the goal and Trinity began to relax a little.

Midway through the half they scored a fortunate try when Topliss made another superb break and passed to Marston. The centre could not hold the pass but fly-kicked the ball to the line and beat the Huddersfield defenders for the touch-down.

Neil Fox finished the scoring with an easy penalty and Trinity ended as comfortable winners.

Major, the ex-Huddersfield wing man, had a great game:

> *... in the first half he was stopped almost on the line and looked a certain scorer when he sent two defenders the wrong way but slipped when he was in the clear.*

Trinity ended the season in ninth position with 21 victories from their 34 games. In the play-off they lost 13–18 to Rochdale Hornets at the Athletic Grounds.

Wakefield Trinity

Wraith, Smith, Marston, Hegarty, Major, Topliss, Harkin (Hawley), Jeanes, Morgan, Lyons, Harrison (Spencer), Valentine, N. Fox

Tries: Topliss 3, Marston

Goals: N. Fox 5

Hat-trick hero David Topliss embarks on a typical darting run.

Huddersfield

Wallace, Hooson, Bedford (Evans), Pickup, Senior, Chamberlain, Doyle, Weavill, Wilson, Davies, Forster, Chawner, Naylor

Goals: Davies, Wallace

Attendance: 3,530

A fine win

League match at Belle Vue, 1 October 1972
Wakefield Trinity 13, Leeds 12

Leeds and Wakefield had both begun the 1972–73 season at a marvellous pace. The Loiners had won their first six games and Trinity had lost just two of their opening fixtures.

The Leeds side possessed a superb back division and their open style of play had led to 45 tries in their first six games.

Wakefield were a vastly improved side and their forwards were developing into a formidable pack, well capable of dictating the way games were played.

Despite their skilful backs Leeds came to Belle Vue intent on taking the game to Trinity down the centre of the field. These proved to be poor tactics, for although Bill Ramsey gave Trinity huge problems with his driving forays in attack, Wakefield held firm and soaked up everything thrown at them. David Jeanes made an unhappy return to his old ground: the huge prop was involved in some very fiery challenges with his old teammates and he often lost possession at critical times.

Over the years, games between Trinity and Leeds have usually provided controversial incidents and this League fixture was to supply another after just five minutes of play.

The Wakefield players were so convinced that a Clawson penalty attempt had gone wide that they began to line up on the 25-yard line, but referee Brown signalled a goal.

Trinity had chance to make amends 10 minutes later when they were awarded a penalty, but Fox's kick was wide.

Midway through the half Trinity took the lead when Topliss found a gap from Fox's pass and managed to cut through before handing on to Bonnar, who then beat three Leeds men to the line. Fox converted and play went from end to end with Barends coming close for Wakefield.

Leeds attacked again and there seemed to be little danger when Hepworth was tacked by Sheard a good 30 yards out. A brilliant play the ball saw the ball transferred to the charging Hardisty, who sprinted over unopposed for a great try. Clawson's fine goal edged Leeds into a slim lead.

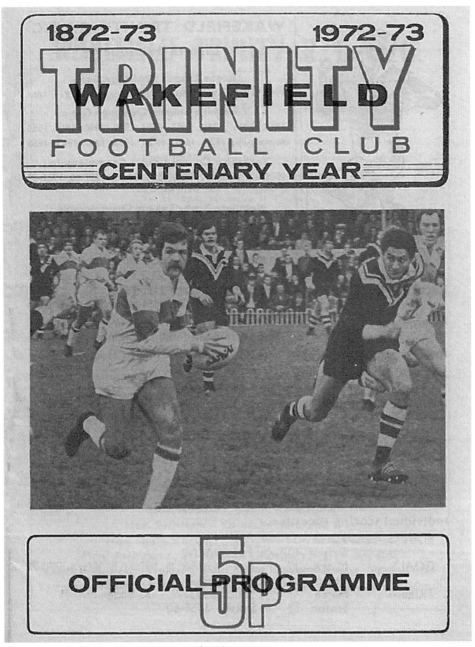

The cover of the Trinity programme for the game.

Almost on half-time Trinity regained the lead when Fox dummied his way through a group of players to create a fine gap and then passed to Wraith in support. The centre took the pass well and completely wrong-footed the cover when he turned inside to score near the posts. Fox missed the kick, but Trinity changed ends with a one-point lead.

Leeds substituted Fisher for Clawson in the second half and Holmes assumed the goal-kicking duties, missing his first three attempts.

Trinity soon extended their lead with a superb long-range try:

> *After Fox had begun the move near his own line, Sheard, who never missed an opportunity to join an attack, sold a classic dummy to open up a big gap in the Leeds defence. He served Barends at halfway and the winger easily outpaced the cover to score in the corner.*

Holmes pulled two points back for Leeds when he kicked a penalty following Lyons's obstruction on Hepworth in front of the posts.

Atkinson fouled Crook and Fox kicked a superb goal from a difficult angle to give Trinity a four-point lead and seemingly a memorable victory.

Three minutes into injury time Leeds won a scrum 10 yards inside the Wakefield half, and with a planned move Holmes launched a huge kick to the corner. Les Dyl had anticipated the kick well and he won the race for the touchdown.

With the final kick of the match Holmes kicked the conversion attempt wide. Wakefield had won by just one point.

Wakefield ended the season in fifth place with 25 victories from their 34 games. In the Championship play-off they defeated Widnes 33–6 at Belle Vue, then lost at St Helens.

Wakefield Trinity

Sheard, Major, Wraith, Crook, Barends, Topliss, Bonnar, Oswald, Handforth, Lyons, Fox, Spencer (Knowles), Morgan

Tries: Bonnar, Wraith, Barends

Goals: Fox 2

Leeds

Nicholls, Langley, Holmes, Dyl, Atkinson, Hardisty, Hepworth, Clawson (Fisher), Ward, Jeanes, Eccles, Ramsey (Pickup), Batten

Tries: Hardisty, Dyl

Goals: Clawson 2, Holmes

Attendance: 8,041

A dramatic victory

Challenge Cup semi-final at Headingley, 7 April 1979
St Helens 7, Wakefield Trinity 9

Trinity conjured up a victory in the face of almost certain defeat with a dramatic last-minute try that sent their supporters wild with excitement.

With just four minutes remaining and with Wakefield 6–4 in the lead, Les Jones, the Saints wing man, crossed for a try to ease St Helens into a single-point lead. Interviewed by Ray Fletcher of the *Yorkshire Post* after the match, Dave Topliss said:

> *I could have wept when Jones scored that try. I really thought that was the end of my Wembley dream. All I could think of is that it was up to me or Keith Smith to produce something special. I told Keith to follow me and when the chance came we took it.*

The chance came almost immediately when Topliss, Smith and Fletcher combined to produce one of the most famous tries in the history of Wakefield Trinity and the Challenge Cup competition. In a final act of inspirational play, Topliss broke free from the St Helens cover and from his own 25-yard line raced to the halfway line. The stand-off transferred to the supporting Smith and the centre swept down the Headingley pitch before passing perfectly to Fletcher, who sprinted in for a dramatic try.

Trinity had given themselves a massive psychological boost the previous week when they defeated St Helens 23–3 at Belle Vue. Wakefield ran in five tries and after 18 minutes had scored 18 points, with Topliss and Lampowski completely overshadowing the visitors Holding and Francis.

At Headingley Trinity's half-back duo were on top form again:

Mike Lampowski moves in to tackle Harry Pinner as the Saints' half-back takes off from the base of the scrum. Trevor Skerrett watches the action from the pack.

> *Topliss stamped his class all over the game, he was the rapier, Lampowski the bludgeon. The Trinity scrum half made no pretence at subtlety. He threw himself at the St Helens defence and repeatedly smashed it.*

Interviewed after the match Lampowski made the following comment:

> *I'm shattered. What a match – the hardest I've played in. When I played Rugby Union Wembley didn't mean anything to me – I've never been as a spectator, I thought Rugby League was a mugs game, now it's marvellous.*

Trinity scored the first try when hooker Alan McCurrie launched a speculative kick towards the Saints try line, and when Glynn missed the ball Fletcher followed up perfectly and pounced on the loose ball. Afterwards McCurrie said of the kick:

> *Did I mean to put the ball through for Fletcher's try? Of course I did. The idea was to put the ball over the St Helens try line and pin them down, but a try was always possible. Fletcher did a great job to get to it.*

Andrew Fletcher recalled the try:

> *McCurrie's kick was spot on, but I couldn't believe when Glynn missed the ball. I was following up fast and somehow ended up sitting down. I turned round and there was the ball.*

Former England RU international Keith Smith kicked one goal and then managed somehow to make the time to land a cool 35-yard drop-goal in the midst of the furious game. For St Helens Les Jones had a superb game, as did Nicholls and Eric Chisnall. Mathias scored the Saints' first try and Pinner dropped a goal.

Trevor Skerrett was voted the man of the match, but Burke, Idle and Keith Rayne were close seconds with superb, hard-working displays on attack and in defence.

Wakefield Trinity

Sheard, (Midgley), Fletcher, Smith, Diamond, Tinker, Topliss, Lampowski, Burke, McCurrie, Skerrett, Keith Rayne, Idle, McDermott (Gregory)

Tries: Fletcher 2

Goals: Smith 2

St Helens

Glynn, Jones, Francis,(Noonan), Cunningham, Mathias, Holding, Gwilliam, D. Chisnall, (Hope), Liptrot, James, Nicholls, E. Chisnall, Pinner

Tries: Mathias, Jones

Goal: Pinner

Attendance: 11,871

A disappointing final

Challenge Cup final at Wembley, 5 May 1979
Wakefield Trinity 3, Widnes 12

Trinity were rank outsiders to take the Cup, with the pundits pointing to their narrow semi-final win and a 50-point trouncing by Bradford the week before the final.

In a dour, defence-dominated game, Wakefield took some solace from the performance of their captain David Topliss. Wakefield were by far the more adventurous team, but as many other sides had found during the season it takes a lot to wear down a Widnes side intent on winning.

The first half was a scoreless battle of attrition between the two packs of forwards, occasionally brought to life by *'The unquenchable artistry of Topliss, a couple of relieving kicks by Ashurst, first left then right, that were judged to a nicety.'*

Stand-off Topliss was playing the game of his life. He tirelessly roamed the field, constantly searching for a way through the awesome blanket defence Widnes had set up. His creative running and endless attempts to coax the best from his side were a joy to watch and brought welcome relief from the constant bone-jarring tackles from the forwards.

The deadlock was broken in the 49th minute when Mick Burke kicked a penalty awarded for a Bill Ashurst indiscretion against Eric Hughes.

Twenty minutes into the half the game exploded into life when:

> *Wright took hold of Wakefield and shook the very breath out of them. Receiving possession in his own half, Wright surged irrepressibly forward. His run took him into enemy territory.*

Wright kicked the ball towards the corner and in a superb and thrilling sprint he beat Diamond and Sheard to the ball for a try. Burke landed the goal from the touchline and Widnes

The dejection of defeat is etched vividly on the faces of David Topliss, Graham Idle and Andrew Fletcher as they descend the famous Wembley steps.

were seven points in the lead. Elwell extended the advantage with a drop goal four minutes later.

Trinity retaliated well, and when a routine move seemed to be drawing to a scoreless conclusion, Keith Rayne chipped the ball forward and Fletcher, eager for the opening, nipped round Burke and scored. Smith missed the conversion.

The comeback was brief, and with 10 minutes to play Eckersley dropped a goal before Hughes feigned to kick and launched himself on a 20-yard curving run to score a clever try.

It was the final score; the expert's predictions had been correct. For David Topliss the match had a been a bitter disappointment but also a personal triumph when his performance earned him the Lance Todd trophy for man of the match.

The *Guardian* summed up his performance during the match:

Dave Topliss, an inspirational captain, won the Lance Todd Trophy as man of the match, for his running, weaving, ducking, and all round creativity and boundless energy.

Wakefield Trinity

Sheard, Fletcher, Smith, Diamond, Juliff, Topliss, Lampowski, Burke, McCurrie, Skerrett, Ashurst, Keith Rayne, Idle

Try: Fletcher

Widnes

Eckersley, Wright, Aspey, George (Hull), Burke, Hughes, Bowden, Mills, Elwell, Shaw, Adams, Dearden, (O'Neill), Laughton

Tries: Wright, Hughes

Goals: Burke, Elwell (drop), Eckersley (drop)

Attendance: 94,218

McCurrie is scoring ace for Trinity

League game at the Athletic Grounds, Rochdale, 7 May 1979

Rochdale Hornets 3, Wakefield Trinity 23

In the space of a few weeks in April and May 1979 Wakefield Trinity's players, officials and supporters witnessed the pinnacle of success, the adoration that goes with it, and the very depths of despair. The breathtaking last-minute victory over St Helens in the Challenge Cup semi-final at Headingley brought a fresh hope and new expectations. People everywhere who were connected with the club were jubilant and enthusiastic. Yet in the Challenge Cup Final at Wembley those hopes were dashed with the defeat by Widnes.

On the Monday following the Final Trinity still had a League fixture with Rochdale Hornets to complete and it was a credit to the professionalism of the officials and players involved at the time that Wakefield held their heads high and played, in the circumstances, a great game.

Smith, Burke, Ashurst and Idle were missing from the Wembley line-up and Midgley came in to the team for Sheard, who was on the substitutes' bench.

Conditions were appalling, with the pitch resembling a swamp in places, vastly different from the lush turf of Wembley. Despite the conditions Trinity played some fine, open football, especially in the first half.

Cumbrian Alan McCurrie was the star for Trinity. The hooker heeled cleanly from eight of the eleven first scrums, taking six in succession. In the loose he backed everything that moved forward and his eager support play earned him a hat-trick of tries.

Trinity opened the scoring in the 11th minute when Trevor Skerrett blasted his way through the Rochdale line. His pass was deflected but McCurrie scooped up the ball to score. Diamond converted. Three minutes later the Hornets were broken again by Skerrett, who passed to Keith Rayne, who ran wide around the full-back to score in the corner. Diamond added the points

144

Trinity's hat-trick star, Cumbrian hooker Alan McCurrie.

with a superb kick. Skerrett was unstoppable; his charging runs created havoc in the Rochdale defence. From another strong burst he tore through the flimsy defence and passed to McCurrie, who followed his own clever little kick to score his second try, which Diamond failed to convert.

Rochdale made a rare incursion into the Wakefield half which broke down in the corner. Topliss collected the ball, fractured the Hornets' first line of defence and then spun a superbly timed pass to the rampaging Skerrett. The second-row man charged through and handed to the supporting McCurrie, who sprinted over the line for his hat-trick. Diamond kicked the goal and Trinity were 18 points in front after just 30 minutes of play.

Five minutes before the interval Wainwright, the Rochdale centre, was sent off for a foul on Fletcher and minutes later their Welsh international Woods limped off to be replaced by McGiffen.

Murray replaced Keith Rayne for the second half, and in the 48th minute Sheard came off the bench for Lampowski, who retired with an arm injury.

Rochdale hooker Langan heeled well in the second half and the Hornets came more into the game. On the hour Birdsall crossed for a try, which Holland failed to convert when he hit the upright. Soon after Trinity were awarded a penalty at a scrum and Thompson ran superbly to set up a good position. Needham wrong-footed the Rochdale defence with a clever dummy at the play the ball and raced 20 yards for a try which Diamond converted.

It was the final score of the match: Wakefield had shown great character to complete their first 'double' of the season.

Wakefield Trinity

Midgley, Fletcher, Needham, Diamond, Juliff, Topliss, Lampowski, (Sheard), Kirkbride, McCurrie, Bratt, Skerrett, Rayne (Murray), Thompson

Tries: McCurrie 3, Rayne, Needham

Goals: Diamond 4

Rochdale Hornets

O'Loughlin, Holland, Fletcher, Wainwright, Johnson, Ayres, Woods (McGiffen), Cooke, Langan, Golding, Garside, Rathbone, (Hodkinson), Birdsall

Try: Birdsall

Attendance: 850.

Lewis and Bell are winners

League game at Belle Vue, 8 January 1984
Wakefield Trinity 31, St Helens 22

Wakefield gained promotion to the Slalom Lager Championship in 1982–83 season with an impressive 25 wins from their 32 fixtures. They began the season in style with a superb 18-14 victory over Fulham, but then began to flounder until early October brought back-to-back wins over Leigh and Featherstone Rovers.

Trinity were desperate to 'stay up' and caused a sensation when they announced they had signed the Australian Test star Wally Lewis for a mid-season stint at Belle Vue.

The Queenslander, who had starred in the 1982 Kangaroos tour, was allegedly paid £1000 a match.

Lewis made his debut for Trinity at Belle Vue against Hull in early December but, despite some wonderful glimpses of his astounding skills, he was overshadowed by Peter Sterling, Hull's debutant Australian half-back.

Two victories and two defeats followed, and then came the visit to Belle Vue of St Helens, who had trounced Trinity 50–12 in late September.

At Leigh the previous week, Wakefield had played Nigel Bell, a young scrum-half from local amateur club Eastmoor. The *Wakefield Express* commented:

> *Just four weeks ago Bell was playing local amateur rugby but on the evidence of Sunday's performance he looks to be the best signing made by Trinity for a long, long time. Bell was always in the thick of the action where he used his strength to great effect on both attack and defence. He regularly brought down forwards in full flight and his fine covering often saved his side from embarrassment.*

Lewis and Bell formed a deadly partnership at half-back, the Australian's subtle mix of power and pace blending perfectly with the raw, explosive style of Bell.

Wakefield opened the scoring when Stephenson drove the ball in near the Saints' line before passing to Bell, who crossed despite being held by a couple of tacklers. Maskill added the conversion.

Rule kicked a penalty awarded by French referee Pourret against Wally Lewis for holding down in a tackle. Then, in a hectic six minute spell, St Helens ripped Trinity open to score 14 points. Haggerty, Allen and Ledger, with an 80-yard sprint, crossed for tries and Rule landed a solitary goal.

Wakefield hit back when Wally Lewis crashed over for two close-range tries, one of which Maskill converted to draw level. Just before the break Saints took full advantage of some terrible Trinity tackling and Platt stormed in for a try which Rule added the two points to with a good kick.

Three minutes into the second half Lewis:

> *... showed his class by completing his hat trick with a dazzling run. He swept through Peters and Smith and then sped away from Rule before touching down.*

Wakefield Trinity, 1983–84 season. Back row: Adams, Box, Gill, Maskill, Bratt, Geary, Harris, Bell, Williams. Front row: Swann, Fletcher, Lewis, Stephenson, Coventry, Jones. The mascot is J. Fairhurst.

Maskill kicked the goal, and then added two more points with a penalty to put Trinity into a 24–22 lead. Minutes later, Bell:

> *... took a pass from the Aussie stand off, broke the first wave of tacklers and then raced 55 yards, crashing through Rule's last ditch effort on a blockbusting run to the line.*

In the last minutes of the game tempers frayed and eventually Geary and Burke were sent to the sin bin for fighting.

The fine win and precious points lifted the club and its supporters, but two defeats at Warrington and Leeds followed. Trinity collected their final two points of the campaign with a victory over Featherstone Rovers in mid-February then lost their final eight games to finish in 14th position and, once again, were relegated.

The decision to sign Wally Lewis had been a brave, but ultimately irrelevant, attempt to keep top-flight Rugby League football at Belle Vue.

Wakefield Trinity

Box, Jones (S. Lewis), Coventry, S. Lewis (Adams), Eden, W. Lewis, Bell, Bratt, Maskill, Waugh, Worne, Geary, Stephenson (Swann)

Tries: W. Lewis 3, Bell 2

Goals: Maskill 5, 1 drop

St Helens

Rule, Ledger, Allen, Haggerty, Litherland, Peters, Smith, Grimes (Round), Liptrot, Burke, Platt, Gorley, Pinner

Tries: Haggerty, Allan, Ledger, Platt

Goals: Rule 3

Attendance: 3,691

Sensational first win by Trinity

League match at Belle Vue, 15 March 1987

Wakefield Trinity 38, Widnes 20

Wakefield's 1986–87 season in the Stones Bitter Championship was a far from happy one, with very few high points. Following three straight League defeats, Trinity defeated Batley in the first round of the Yorkshire Cup. They lost in the second round to Hull and then were defeated in seven consecutive League games. Brief respite came with a victory over amateurs Millom in the John Player Special Trophy and a 14-all draw against Barrow at Belle Vue, before another run of eight defeats.

A 15–10 Challenge Cup victory at Blackpool brought some relief and confidence back to the club and then, following defeats at Whitehaven, Featherstone, Salford and Warrington, Widnes came to Belle Vue.

Trinity were expected to win some of their League games, but not even their most optimistic followers could have envisaged Trinity's sensational drubbing of high-flying Widnes. The *Wakefield Express* commented:

> *No side could have coped with Wakefield as they played some brilliant rugby. Panic became the key word as Widnes faltered under extreme pressure, and in their attempts to break clear of Trinity's stranglehold they made mistake after mistake, which with great calmness and confidence Wakefield turned into points.*

Widnes took the lead in third minute when Sorenson and McKenzie created an opening for full-back Platt to score a fine try. The small crowd of onlookers must have thought 'here we go again', another league defeat. Trinity had other ideas and following a penalty goal from Kevin

Nigel Bell, who made 23 appearances during the season scoring five tries.

Harcombe, Gary Cocks and John Lyons sent Steve Halliwell over for his first try for the club. Harcombe kicked the goal and the crowd began to stir into life. With 15 minutes gone:

> *Cocks again made the important move with a cut back to the line before sending*
> *Nigel Bell over for a try and Harcombe hit goal number three.*

Minutes later Wakefield won a scrum against the head, Bell delayed his pass to Sheldon to perfection and the second-row man was over for a try which Harcombe converted. Wakefield's tackling was fearsome, with Cocks, Douglas, and debutant Jasiewicz pounding into the Widnes players with such ferocity that they spilled the ball at an alarming rate.

Widnes were gaining ample possession from the scrums but the pressure of the Wakefield defence was creating havoc with their rhythm. Under pressure Linton threw out a wild pass that Klein intercepted to score Trinity's fourth try. Harcombe kicked the goal then landed a penalty to make it six from six. On the stroke of half time Klein ran straight through Widnes full-back

Platt to score a great try in the corner, and from an acute angle Harcombe kicked his seventh goal to give Trinity an unbelievable 34–4 half-time lead.

Widnes coach Dougie Laughton made two changes at half time and Widnes pulled back slightly when Stockley sent Wright in for a try which Platt converted. With their confidence at its highest point of the season, Wakefield were in no mood to give in and on the hour Sheldon put Phil Eden in for a try.

Trinity eventually tired a little and in the final six minutes Linton and Dowd scored tries to give Widnes a little respectability to the score line. But it was Wakefield's afternoon and their proud followers gave the team a rousing cheer as the final whistle went.

Wakefield won three more games, including a double over Halifax, and were relegated with just nine points to show from their 30 games.

———————

Wakefield Trinity

Harcombe, Klein, Halliwell, Eden, Rotherforth, Lyons, Bell, Van Bellen, Conway, Cocks, (Hopkinson), Jasiewicz, Douglas, Sheldon, (N. Kelly)

Tries: Klein 2, Halliwell, Bell, Sheldon, Eden

Goals: Harcombe 7

Widnes

Platt, Dowd, Wright, Linton, Thackray, D. Hulme, Sullivan, Sorenson, McKenzie, M. O'Neill, Newton, Eyres, (Stockley), Pinner (P. Hulme)

Tries: Wright, Linton, Dowd, Platt

Goals: Platt 2

Attendance: 1,613

Hard-earned Cup cheer for Trinity

Yorkshire Challenge Cup second round at Belle Vue, 2 September 1990

Wakefield Trinity 26, Halifax 17

Trinity began their Cup campaign with a 28–18 victory over second division Hunslet, who, early in the second half, were leading by four points. Fallen giants Halifax then came to Belle Vue with great confidence, having trounced Doncaster by 36 points at Tattersfield.

Trinity made three changes to the side which beat Halifax; Perry switched to the wing to allow Lazenby to play stand-off and new club captain Andy Kelly went back into the second row.

Halifax took the lead in the sixth minute when former Trinity half-back, John Lyons, dropped a clever goal, and four minutes later Alan Platt landed a superb penalty goal.

Trinity responded well and with a little help from an upright opened their scoring when:

> *Mark Conway wriggled free of a posse of defenders on the Halifax quarter line, but, seemed to have over – hit his grubber kick through. However, the ball struck the upright allowing Conway to win a race to the ball and Harcombe landed a simple conversion.*

Harcombe's boot stretched the lead eight minutes later when he landed a penalty, awarded when Andy Walker was flattened by a high tackle. Andy Walker, the Trinity hooker, was always in the thick of the action and following a brief altercation with Jason Ramshaw, both players were sent to the sin bin.

Wakefield should have scored a try soon after when Conway, Price and Kelly created the best move of the game, but with the line beckoning Harcombe lost the ball. Three minutes later

Mark Conway, opening try scorer for Trinity.

Halifax showed a glimpse of class when loose-forward Wood fashioned a gap for Hutchinson to sprint through. The Halifax centre sped down the field and passed to Wilf George, who just beat the cover to score a fine try.

Five minutes before the break, Nigel Bell came on for Steve Potts and immediately helped set up a good field position. Kelly and Slater came close to scoring, and then John Thompson forced his way over for an important try before half-time. Harcombe converted from a difficult angle.

> *Thompson, whose rare tries last season included cup-tie efforts against Swinton and Sheffield, fully deserved his score for an unstinting first half effort.*

Halifax pulled two points back with a penalty from Platt but once again extended their lead. A huge kick from Conway had Halifax in deep trouble and Perry almost scored in the corner. From a scrum Trinity were awarded a penalty, and a superb long pass from Walker gave Price the room to dive over for a good try. Harcombe converted.

Halifax refused to concede and continued to worry the Trinity defence and after a spell of pressure Ramshaw found George with a clever pass for the wing man's second try. Trinity and their followers were relieved to see Platt's kick drift wide of the posts. With around 20 minutes remaining, Conway launched a superb kick into the heart of the Halifax defence. Price followed the kick well and, gaining possession, transferred to Jones, who gave the ball quickly to Kelly, who tore across the line for a superb try. Harcombe landed his fifth goal of the match with his well-struck conversion.

Wakefield looked safe, but once again their defence faltered and allowed a tenacious Halifax side a faint hope of victory. Slack marking and hesitant tackling gave the impressive Halifax loose forward Wood the chance to break clear in the middle of the field and race in for a good try.

It was the final score of the game and, despite some fundamental mistakes in defence, Trinity were through to their first County Cup semi-final since 1974.

In the semi-final at Belle Vue, Wakefield trounced Dewsbury 25–2 to set up their first Yorkshire Cup final for 16 years.

Wakefield Trinity

Harcombe, Perry, Mason, Eden, Jones, Lazenby, M. Conway, Potts (Bell), Walker, Thompson, Kelly, Price, Slater (A. Wilson)

Tries: M. Conway, Thompson, Price, Kelly

Goals: Harcombe 5

Halifax

Smith, Atkinson (P. Bell), A.N. Other (Needham), Hutchinson, George, Southernwood, Lyons, Scott, Ramshaw, Fairbank, Platt, Keebles, Wood

Tries: George 2, Wood

Goals: Platt 2, Lyons

Attendance: 6,492

A controversial final

Yorkshire Challenge Cup final at Headingley, 23 September 1990
Castleford 11, Wakefield Trinity 8

Trinity were making their first Yorkshire Cup Final appearance since 1974, when they lost 16–13 to Hull Kingston Rovers at Headingley. For Castleford it was their seventh appearance in 10 seasons.

Wakefield coach David Topliss had predicted that if outsiders Trinity could hold the free-flowing Castleford attack in the first 20 minutes, they would be in with a chance.

In the event they did far more than that, for in the fifth minute Tracey Lazenby, from a scrum near the halfway line, broke clear in superb arcing run, then passed to Mason who scored a superb try. Harcombe scored the goal from an acute angle and Trinity found themselves with a six-point lead.

Four minutes later Atkins dummied his over for a good, unconverted try, but Castleford still looked unsettled. Wakefield's defence managed to hold firm and Harcombe extended their lead with a penalty that came just before the interval.

Early in the second half Lazenby sliced the Castleford defence wide open and spun a slick pass to Andy Mason. Mason was within inches of a certain try when Plange, playing in his first game of the season, sprinted across to cut the centre down with a superb tackle.

Lee Crooks eventually cut Trinity's lead back with a well-struck penalty, and then, in the 63rd minute, Castleford took the lead in controversial circumstances.

Battye and Ellis carved open the Trinity defence down the right, then switched play across the field to Southernwood, who flung a pass to Plange, who charged over the line in the corner. Plange knocked over the corner flag and the Trinity players claimed that Plange had made a double movement to score. Halifax referee Jim Smith would have none of the protests and gave a try; he later said:

Tracey Lazenby, whose superb display gave him the man of the match award.

I saw his hand on the ball over the line, checked with the touch judge and was satisfied he had scored.

After the game, although disappointed, Trinity coach David Topliss agreed with the referee's decision.

Trinity continued to attack Castleford but apart from some skilful touches from Lazenby, their route down the centre of the field had little impact on their opponents.

In the final seconds of the game Neil Roebuck dropped a goal for Castleford to give them a three-point victory.

Wakefield gained some consolation when Tracey Lazenby was awarded the the White Rose trophy for man of the match.

Wakefield Trinity

Harcombe, Jones, Mason, Eden, Wilson, Lazenby, M. Conway, Shelford, B. Conway (Salter), Thompson, Kelly (Perry), Price, Bell

Try: Mason

Goals: Harcombe 2

Castleford

Larder, Ellis, Irwin, Anderson, Plange, Steadman, Atkins (England), Crookes, Southernwood, Sampson, Battye (Ketteridge), Hardy, Roebuck

Tries: Atkins, Plange

Goals: Crooks, Roebuck

Attendance: 12,420

Battered and bloodied Trinity celebrate winning the last-ever Yorkshire Challenge Cup final.

Final victory for Trinity

Yorkshire Challenge Cup final at Elland Road, Leeds, 18 October 1992
Wakefield Trinity 29, Sheffield Eagles 16

Trinity began the last-ever Yorkshire Cup campaign in fine style when they ran in 10 tries to rout Doncaster 54–14 at Belle Vue in the first round, then defeated a tough Keighley side 22–16, to secure a semi-final berth with an injury-time try from Gary Spencer. A visit to Featherstone in the semi brought a 22–8 win, the home side losing Brendan Tuuta, who was sent off just before the half-time break.

The Eagles started their cup quest with a 34–14 home defeat of Halifax, thanks to a hat-trick of tries from David Plange and a touch down from Australian Test full-back Gary Jack. It was in-form Plange who helped the Eagles beat Bradford Northern in the next round, the wing man coasting in for a brace of tries at Odsal. Sheffield scored a memorable victory over Hull in the semi, despite being behind after a Lee Jackson try after just nine seconds.

A disappointing crowd of just less than 8,000 witnessed Sheffield's first and Trinity's 20th Yorkshire Cup Final.

Trinity had a dream start when, in the fifth minute, a Nigel Wright kick-through caught a defender's foot and ricocheted into the arms of Richard Slater, who swept round Australian full-back Gary Jack for a try which Peter Benson converted.

Eighteen-year-old Wright dropped a goal in the 16th minute and two minutes later Wakefield's Aussie captain Geoff Bagnall stole over for a try after he hoodwinked the Eagles' defence with a quick tap penalty.

The game was as good as over within five minutes of the second half starting, when Nigel Wright conjured up two flashes of pure class.

A superb angled run cut clean through the Eagles' midfield and a shrewd side-step and perfect pass fashioned a try under the sticks for Gary Spencer. Within minutes Wright struck again when, gripped by a seemingly perfect tackle, the stand-off slipped a pass to Andy Mason and the centre raced over for a try.

In the 50th minute and trailing 21–0 the Eagles finally contributed to the game when Aussie Bruce McGuire scored two swift tries which Mycoe converted.

The brief Sheffield comeback soon disintegrated when another clever run from Wright saw a penalty awarded when the Eagles' defence held the big stand-off far too long in the tackle. Benson kicked the penalty and added another goal when Gary Price scored a good try after a surging run from a play the ball by Billy Conway.

Despite being well beaten Sheffield kept going to the end and scored a fine try when Mark Gamson beat two men in a final flourish down the right-hand touchline.

Trinity's victory was fashioned from the front of the pack with props Mark Webster and John Glancy punching holes and creating time and space for half-backs Nigel Bell and Geoff Bagnall to control the game with a mixture of piercing runs and delicate passes.

Trinity's teenage sensation Nigel Wright won the coveted White Rose Trophy for the man of the match to become the youngest-ever recipient of the award in his first-ever final.

Wakefield Trinity

Spencer, Jones, Mason, Benson, Wilson, Wright, Bagnall, Webster, Bell, Glancy, Price, Fritz, Slater, Goddard, Conway

Tries: Slater, Bagnall, Spencer, Mason, Price

Goals: Benson 3. Wright 2

Sheffield Eagles

Jack, Gamson, Price, Mycoe, Plange, Aston, Lumb, Broadhead, Cook, Laughton, McGuire, Carr, Farrell, Young, Waddell

Tries: McGuire 2, Gamson

Goals: Mycoe 2

Attendance: 7,918

Trinity strength sinks Rovers

First Division Grand Final at McAlpine Stadium, Huddersfield,
26 September 1998

Featherstone Rovers 22, Wakefield Trinity 24

The inaugural First Division Grand Final gave the crowd everything: a superb game, a tremendous spectacle and for Wakefield Trinity the reward for a long and gruelling season. Wakefield's power in the pack gave them the edge on a Rovers side that had pace and flair. Trinity coach Andy Kelly commented after the emotional game:

> *I would like to pay tribute to Featherstone. I don't think as a team they could have done any more than they did and I thought Richard Chapman was a deserving man of the match. The turning point was our final try, because there were no certainties until then, with perhaps our spirit and strength of commitment eventually seeing us through. But I wouldn't have liked extra time. That would have been a nightmare.*

Trinity took the lead in the second minute when Roy Southernwood darted over from a quick play the ball near the Featherstone line. Four minutes later Australian Bostock ran straight through Hall to score in the corner. Rovers hit back with a try from Danny Baker which Chapman converted. Bostock, Trinity's huge wing man, scored again when he powered his way past Hall.

At half-time it was 12–6 to Wakefield, but within minutes of the restart Rovers hit back in style. Chico Jackson crossed from close range and then Steve Collins finished a superb break from scrum-half Fallins to give Featherstone the lead. Chapman converted both tries to give Featherstone a six-point lead.

A try and a goal from Casey levelled the scores but Featherstone once again took the game to Wakefield and a well-worked move put Hall in at the corner. With a four-point lead and 10 minutes to play Featherstone seemed to have done enough to win the game. Trinity dug deep into a seam of stamina and ambition and began a final breathtaking onslaught. Their Australian captain Matt Fuller said after the game:

> *This was as intense as anything I experienced in Australia and as big as any game I have played in. After Featherstone's last try I had to give my players a bit of a blasting and ask them to lift their intensity for one more effort with something like ten minutes to go. We did that and held like champions.*

The drama continued when Asa Amone grabbed a loose ball in his own half and flashed through the Wakefield cover before transferring to Pratt, who touched down amid scenes of wild emotion. The Featherstone joy was short-lived, however, as referee Oddy brought the play back for a knock-on Amone had committed when gathering the ball. From the scrum Trinity worked the ball to wing man Francis Stephenson to score a superb try. With two minutes remaining and the scores locked at 22–22, stand-off Garen Casey coolly kicked the goal to put Trinity into a two-point lead and Super League 1999.

The disappointed but proud Featherstone coach Steve Simms said after the match:

> *I said to my players straight after the match that I was immensely proud of them, and though they were losers in the game they were not losers as people. I think if Wakefield get everything in order off the field they should be promoted. I don't think they are too far behind the other Super League clubs if you take away the first half dozen.*

Wakefield's victory earned them the right to apply for promotion to Super League and after a series of deliberations they were admitted to begin a rollercoaster ride of amazing highs and lows in the domestic game's premier competition.

Wakefield Trinity

Holland, Gray, M. Law, A Hughes, Bostock, Casey, Kenworthy, Stephenson, Southernwood, Lord, I. Hughes, Whakarau, Fuller

Substitutes: Fisher, Richardson, McDonald

Tries: Southernwood, Bostock 2, Casey, Stephenson

Goals: Casey 2

Featherstone Rovers

Collins, Hall, Irwin, Baker, Pratt, Coventry, Fallins, Jackson, Chapman, Dickens, Price, Lowe, Slater

Substitutes: Amone, Clarkson, Handley

Tries: Baker, Jackson, Collins, Hall

Goals: Chapman 3

Attendance: 8,224

Sweet revenge

Super League match at Belle Vue, 12 April 2001
Wakefield Trinity Wildcats 16, Bradford Bulls 12

Wakefield avenged their 38–0 defeat in the Challenge Cup quarter-final early in the season with a superb victory over powerful, title-chasing Bradford.

From the kick-off Bradford's diminutive scrum half Deacon began to cause the Trinity defence countless problems with his probing runs and his superb repertoire of kicks. Within

A characteristic break from Willie Pochin.

minutes he had created a try for his half-back partner Robbie Paul, and then almost put Leon Pryce in with a delicate and accurate cross-field kick.

Wakefield were reeling and everything pointed to yet another humiliating defeat for the hosts.

Robbie Paul ghosted his way through a bemused Trinity defence to find Leon Pryce loitering with intent on the left touchline. His superb spinning pass gave Pryce a simple try. Deacon missed the conversion but Bradford were in a 10-point lead after just 11 minutes of play.

Then Willie Pochin, Trinity's captain, burst through the usually reliable Bradford defence and, storming past halfway, gave the ball to Law, who with a clever run evaded tackles from Spruce and Wilkinson to score a fine try. Martin Pearson gave the Wakefield half of the crowd hope with a superb conversion.

Five minutes later Pearson, sensing that the Bulls' defence had advanced a little too far and a little too early, kicked through the line and regathered. His break gave him the time and space to find Neil Law out wide and Pearson's pass put him over for his second try in five minutes.

Before the interval a Deacon penalty restored Bradford's slender lead.

Wakefield were level again early in the second half when Pearson kicked a penalty. Gradually Wakefield's forwards began to dominate and Bradford began to struggle to contain the eager Trinity pack.

Neil Law crashes over for a try.

Jamie Field came close and then a mass scramble for the ball over the Bradford line saw the visitors forced to drop out.

Wakefield brought on David March and, with his first touch of the ball, the forward beat two defenders with a dummy and powered over for a try. March came near again just minutes later but knocked the ball forward at the crucial moment.

Trinity held on for their second win of the season and Bradford were denied the chance to top the league table.

Wakefield Trinity Wildcats

Holland, N. Law, Smith, Brooker, Sovatabua, Pearson, G. Law, O'Neill, Rauter, Watene, Hudson, Pochin, Field.

Substitutes: D. March, Jackson, Haughey, Mason

Tries: Law 2, March

Goals: Pearson 2

Bradford Bulls

Spruce, Wilkinson, Gilmour, Rigon, R. Paul, Deacon, Vagana, Lowes, McDermott, Peacock, Radford, Forshaw

Substitutes: Fielden, Gartner, Anderson, H. Paul

Tries: R. Paul, Pryce.

Goals: Deacon 2

Attendance: 4,721

Trinity survive the drop

Super League game at the Willows, Salford, 16 September 2002
Salford City Reds 24, Wakefield Trinity Wildcats 32

A tense, dramatic game that saw four players sent off and two others sin-binned gave Trinity the victory they needed to avoid the drop into the Northern Ford Premiership.

The emotional victory was as much about affairs off the pitch as the victory on it. Wakefield, who had been deducted two points following a breach of the salary cap the previous season, finished the season a single point above Huddersfield but were uncertain about their Super League survival. Australian coach John Harbin commented after the match, *'What we've done is put the ball back in their court, and I'm talking about you know who.'* He was referring to the rumours circulating that despite their last-gasp survival the club's off field standards might not reach Super League's minimum standards. Harbin added:

> *People really undervalue the working-class fan. At the moment it's all about people in suits and ties with accountancy degrees, but that lot on our terraces went to the University of Adversity.*

Trinity trailed 18–14 at the half-time break and looked almost certain to be relegated. Hancock, Baynes and Maloney had crossed for Salford in the first half and for Wakefield Gareth Ellis and Willie Pochin scored tries.

Salford extended their lead and deepened Trinity's plight when Littler intercepted a pass on his own line and sprinted the length of the field to put Wakefield 10 points adrift.

Then, in the 52nd minute, the game exploded into all kinds of action. Neil Law scored a try for Trinity, then Stuart Littler tripped Martin Pearson and was sent off by referee Russell Smith. Minutes later Bobby Goulding was sin-binned for deliberate offside and on his way to the dug out he became involved with Jason Brookner. When the dust had settled the pair were sent off.

A Gareth Ellis break is stopped by three Salford players.

On the hour a superb pass from Sovatabua sent Law over for his second try and Pearson's goal made it 26–24 to Wakefield.

Two minutes from time Holroyd was shown the red card for a trip-cum-kick on David March, then deep into stoppage time Trinity sealed survival with a try from David March.

Wakefield's players and their 2,500 travelling supporters went wild with joy as the final hooter was sounded.

Wakefield Trinity Wildcats

N. Law, Sovatabua, Brooker, Ellis, Westwood, Pearson, Davies, O'Neill, D. March, Watene, Field, Pochin, Hudson

Substitutes: Jackson, Price, G. Law, Rauter

Trinity and their followers celebrate the incredible victory.

Tries: Ellis, Pochin, N. Law 2, D. March

Goals: Pearson 5, Davies

Salford City Reds

Arnold, Platt, Maloney, Littler, Hancock, Holroyd, Goulding, Driscoll, Alker, Baynes, Barton, Highton, Wainwright

Substitutes: Makin, Stevens, L. Marsh, Gorski

Tries: Hancock, Baynes, Maloney, Littler

Goals: Holroyd 4

Attendance: 4,264

A 50-point survival spree

Super League match at Belle Vue, 22 September 2002

Wakefield Trinity Wildcats 50, Warrington Wolves 10

For the second season in succession Trinity needed to win their final match of the season to ensure Super League survival. They did it in a style which not even the most optimistic of their loyal followers could have hoped for and inflicted their best-ever victory on a Warrington side.

Wakefield played as if they had not a care in the world and their veteran player-coach Adrian Vowles and captain Brad Davies led from the front to inspire the rest of the team to a dramatic and emotional victory.

Vowles, who was playing centre, his fourth different position for the club, opened the scoring with a superb run that cut through the Warrington defence. Stand-off Brad Davies was at the helm of just about every Trinity attack and his neat running and precision passing brought a try for second-row forward Jamie Field. Minutes later the captain popped up at the right time to take a return pass from his half-back partner Paul Handforth to score himself.

Wakefield were playing with confidence and showing skills and all-round ability that made a mockery of their precocious position in the Super League table.

A high speed and intricate passing movement gave wing man Andrew Frew Trinity's fourth try, and as a contest the game was as good as finished.

Warrington scored a solitary try in the first half when second-row forward Darren Burns burrowed over the line for a try.

Just before half-time Vowles helped himself to his second try when he collected the ball directly from a scrum and raced away for a fine opportunist try.

Wakefield's procession to the line continued on the resumption and a disappointing Warrington put up very little resistance to Trinity's charge forward.

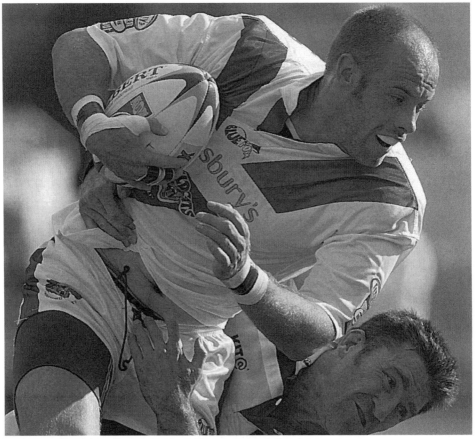

Martin Holland is pulled down by a Warrington defender.

Kris Tassell and Davies pierced the outclassed Warrington defences for fine tries early in the second half.

A brief rally and some shoddy Wakefield defending gave the Warrington scrum-half a try midway through the half. Then Davies fashioned some more openings for Vowles to complete his hat-trick and a 10th try for Chris Feather. Appropriately Adrian Vowles completed the scoring when he converted the final try of the afternoon.

Wakefield's followers went wild with delight at the final hooter but then had an agonising wait until the Salford result was announced. The Reds had lost 14–10 at home to Castleford and they were relegated.

The *Warrington Guardian* commented on the game:

> *Many embarrassing defeats have sunk primrose and blue hearts in Warrington's*
> *worst League season in history but Sunday's mauling at the hands of the Wildcats*

took the biscuit. After securing Super League survival with victories over Halifax and Castleford the Wolves players might as well have put their boots away for the year and gone on their holidays.

Wakefield Trinity Wildcats

Holland, Frew, Vowles, Ellis, Tassell, Handforth, Davies, Jackson, March, Feather, Slattery, Field, Knott

Substitutes: Keating, Broadbent, Wray

Tries: Vowles 3, Field, Davies 3, Frew, Tassell, Feather

Goals: Knott 4, Vowles

Warrington Wolves

Penny, Smyth, Alstead, Westwood, Maden, O'Reilly, Hulse, Stevens, N. Wood, Hilton, P. Wood, Guisset, Burns

Substitutes: Noone, Sturm, Hill, Fozzard

Tries: Burns, Hulse

Goals: Smyth

Attendance: 4,500

The relief shows as Trinity celebrate another incredible victory to stay in the Super League.

Trinity regain pride

Super League match at Belle Vue, 30 August 2003

Wakefield Trinity Wildcats 35, Hull FC 28

The win means a lot to us. We put in one of our worst performances last time we played Hull and the last few games we have been similarly bad. We were looking to fix the ledger up and show the fans what we can do and we did just that.

That is how Trinity coach Shane summed up his side's superb five-try defeat of Hull.

Wakefield's forwards were a domineering force throughout the game and, prompted well by the half-back partnership of Rooney and Jeffries, they created havoc in the Hull defence.

Hull started well and opened the scoring when loose forward play followed a strong run from Yeaman. Trinity hit back and in a mesmerising period tore the Hull side to pieces. Powerful prop Korkidas blasted over the line from a perfect position created by an inch-perfect 40–20 kick from Ben Jeffries. French debutant Sylvain Houles surged forward to set up a try for Wrench and then David March was awarded a penalty try when Smith obstructed his progress to the line. Smith spent 10 minutes in the sin bin for his misdemeanour and on his return Trinity scored again when Handforth's initial surge brought a try for Houles, who supported well.

Hull rallied and before the break Smith and Raynor scored tries.

On the restart Trinity came straight back at Hull and a brilliant move involving Korkidas, Jeffries and Rooney put wing man Matt Wray over. Rooney missed his first kick of the match but later added a couple of penalties to extend the Trinity lead.

Hull scored further tries with Richard Horne and McMenemy crossing, but the boot of Rooney stretched Trinity's lead with a further penalty and a drop.

Hull coach Shaun McRae said after the game:

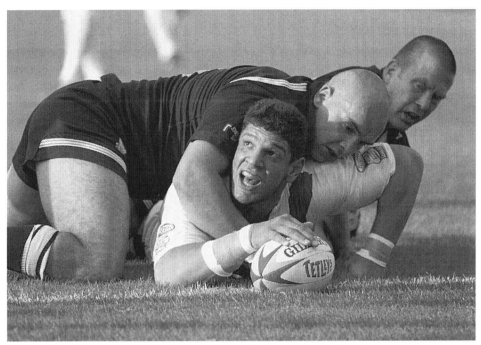

Michael Korkidas shows his delight as he plants the ball over the line.

Frenchman Sylvain Houles scores a fine acrobatic try.

A team which essentially had nothing to play for apart from pride have totally out-enthused us and deserved to win.

Wakefield Trinity Wildcats

Wells, Wray, Houles, Halpenny, Newlove, Rooney, Jeffries, Korkidas, March, Griffin, Wrench, Hood, Field

Substitutes: Holland, Snitch, Handforth, Blake

Tries: Korkidas, Wrench, March, Houles, Wray

Goals: Rooney 8 (one drop)

Hull FC

Wilkinson, Best, Barnett, Yeaman, Raynor, Cooke, R. Horne, Greenhill, Last, Ryan, Chester, Smith,

Substitutes: McMenemy, Lupton, Dowes, Carvell

Tries: Smith 2, Raynor, McMenemy, R. Horne

Goals: Cooke 4

Attendance: 3,689

11313017R00096

Printed in Great Britain
by Amazon